WHY COOLIDGE MATTERS

© 2010 National Notary Association

Published by
The National Notary Association
9350 De Soto Avenue, P.O. Box 4567
Chatsworth, CA 91313-4567

www.NationalNotary.org
email: nna@nationalnotary.org

Publisher's Cataloging-in-Publication Data

Why Coolidge matters : how civility in politics can bring a nation together / compiled by the National Notary Association. — Chatsworth, Calif. : National Notary Association, 2010.

p. ; cm.

ISBN13: 978-1-59767-055-5

1. Coolidge, Calvin, 1872-1933. 2. Presidents–United States–Biography. 3. United States–History–1919-1933. 3. United States–Politics and government–1919-1933. I. Title. II. National Notary Association (U.S.)

E792.W49 2010
973.915—dc22   2010920812

FIRST EDITION

Printed in the United States of America
14 13 12 11 10 • 5 4 3 2 1

the separation
these are Life, Liberty and the
of Government
its powers in
for light

WHY COOLIDGE MATTERS

How Civility in Politics Can Bring a Nation Together

PHOTOGRAPHS COURTESY OF THE
CALVIN COOLIDGE MEMORIAL FOUNDATION
&
THE LIBRARY OF CONGRESS

NATIONAL NOTARY ASSOCIATION

CONTENTS

First lady Grace Coolidge

CONTENTS

ESSAYS

APPENDIX

ACKNOWLEDGMENTS

Careful reflection on American history over the course of a collective hundreds of years of scholarship have produced the penetrating insights, analyses and observations of this book about why Calvin Coolidge, the thirtieth President of the United States, still matters today. Producing a volume of this scope and quality required the commitment of many experts from across the nation. With deep appreciation, the National Notary Association expresses its sincere gratitude to all of those who, in different ways, contributed to this work.

We are most grateful to Cynthia D. Bittinger, the now-retired Executive Director of the Calvin Coolidge Memorial Foundation, for her partnership, guidance and expertise in the development and review of this volume's content. In addition to providing an insightful essay of her own for this volume, Cyndy spent countless hours reviewing the book's text for historical accuracy and consistency — and her acumen proved invaluable in the editing and proofing process. Her hard-working staff also deserves recognition for their perseverance in scouring the Foundation's photographic archive. Many of the rarely seen images they submitted are included in this book.

We would also like to thank the Calvin Coolidge Memorial Foundation's distinguished Board of Trustees. These individuals are ably furthering the Foundation's mission to boost public awareness of President Coolidge's legacy in order to foster a better understanding of our nation's history and thereby forge a stronger American society. Their continued unflagging support and cooperation helped make this book possible.

We are especially fortunate to have assembled a group of widely recognized and influential scholars, historians, media commentators, political leaders, and prominent voices on public issues to contribute their analyses about why Coolidge continues to matter to all Americans today, and why he remains a shining example of what a conscientious and selfless public servant should be. Their essays, which appear in this volume randomly and without any intent on our part to show favor or partiality, explore every aspect of his life, ideals, influence, and legacy.

With the reawakening in recent decades to the historical significance of the Coolidge presidency, the contributions of these distinguished authors — all original works produced specifically for inclusion in this volume — constitute a genuine boon to future scholars and curious citizens alike.

We would like to offer special thanks to the Honorable Jim Douglas, Governor of Vermont, who penned the foreword to this body of work. As a man who is inspired by Coolidge's legacy, and the governor of the state he called home, Douglas provides an insightful analysis about why the nation's thirtieth President still matters today.

We are also grateful and fortunate to have the participation of three prominent and influential political leaders of our generation, each of whom shares President Coolidge's experience of rising to high public office in a New England state: the Honorable Michael Dukakis, former Governor of Massachusetts and 1988 Democratic Presidential nominee; the Honorable John F. Kerry, U.S. Senator from Massachusetts and 2004 Democratic Presidential nominee; and the Honorable M. Jodi Rell, Governor of Connecticut. From their vantage at the highest level of government, these three important voices provide context about how Coolidge's values and ideals would benefit the nation today.

Because dedicated advocacy is critical in the development of public policy, we are pleased to have the contribution of Ward Connerly, author and President of the American Civil Rights Institute. In addition, the essay by J.R. Greene, author and expert on the Coolidge Presidency, is a valuable contribution to this volume.

We were privileged to secure the participation of three gifted writers with special perspectives on the thirtieth president: Amity Shlaes, syndicated columnist and Senior Fellow, Council on Foreign Relations; David M. Shribman, Pulitzer Prize-winning Executive Editor of the Pittsburgh Post-Gazette; and Jerry L. Wallace, historian, writer and retired archivist for the National Archives and Records Administration, Washington, D.C. Their essays detail how Coolidge's beliefs and ideals helped shape the country we inhabit, and how re-embracing them would help restore faith in government.

The essential core of this volume comprises the diverse essays of the nation's top scholars and historians on Coolidge's legacy and the American Presidency. We give special thanks to this prominent group of intellectuals: Robert H. Ferrell, Ph.D., author, historian and retired Professor of History at Indiana University; Alvin S. Felzenberg, Ph.D., author and visiting lecturer at the University of Pennsylvania and George Washington University; Burton Folsom, Jr., Ph.D., Charles Kline Professor of History and Management at Hillsdale College, Michigan; Russell Fowler, J.D., Adjunct Professor of Political Science at the University of Tennessee, Chattanooga; Robert E. Gilbert, Ph.D., Edward W. Brooke Professor of Political Science at Northeastern University; Melanie Gustafson, author, historian and Associate Professor of History at the University of Vermont; Daniel J. Leab, Ph.D., Professor of History at Seton Hall University; John Moser, Ph.D., Associate Professor of History at Ashland University and a U.S. Presidential Scholar; Peter W. Schramm, Ph.D., Executive Director of the John M. Ashbrook Center for Public Affairs and Professor of Political Science at Ashland University; and L. John Van Til, Ph.D., Professor and Visiting Scholar at Harvard University.

Without their authoritative perspectives and analyses of Coolidge's legacy, this book would not constitute the solid contribution to scholarship that it is.

Special acknowledgment is due the Coolidge family for their generosity and public-spiritedness over the years. Particular acknowledgment goes out to the great-grandchildren of President Coolidge — Jennifer Sayles Harville, John Sayles and Christopher Coolidge Jeter — who continue to enable the valuable legacy of our thirtieth President to be shared with the American people.

For the photographic content of this book, we are indebted to the cooperation and vast resources of the Library of Congress. The Library deserves special recognition for helping the NNA illustrate Coolidge's legacy through distinctive and rarely seen photographs that give this book a very special dimension.

We would also like to thank the dedicated staff of the National Notary Association, who collectively spent thousands of hours over more than four years compiling editorial and graphical content, editing, designing and producing this book. Key NNA contributors, led by the book's managing director Phillip W. Browne, included graphic designer Michael D. Suorsa; production manager Michael K. Valera; production coordinator Alice L. Zumstein; production editor Consuelo R. Israelson; associate editor David S. Thun; and publication coordinator Sheryl D. Turner. Vice Presidents William A. Anderson and Steven J. Bastian were particularly instrumental with their executive leadership and counsel. And the overall communications and marketing expertise and general management of Executive Director Michael Robinson were invaluable.

We would like to give very special thanks to the NNA's Executive Vice President Deborah M. Thaw, who also serves as Executive Director of the National Notary Foundation, and Vice President of Notary Affairs Charles N. Faerber, both of whom made critically important contributions in the production of this body of work, from concept to publication. Their combined six decades of service and expertise to the Notary community were without equal in the guidance of this project.

Lastly, this awesome endeavor and the ultimate publication of this book would not have been possible without the vision and leadership of National Notary Association President Milt Valera. As the driving force behind the largest and most recognized organization serving America's more than 4.8 million Notaries, Valera's dedication to publishing this ambitious and comprehensive volume mirrors his commitment of over forty years to serve, educate and professionalize Notaries.

The fundamental motivation for this book — to heighten respect for American democracy — is an effort that supports the educational mission of the National Notary Association. It also gives us all an opportunity to reflect on our future by closely examining the life of President Calvin Coolidge.

INTRODUCTION

COOLIDGE'S LIFE AND VALUES CAN GUIDE US ALL

By MILT VALERA
President of the National Notary Association

Calvin Coolidge was destined to come to the attention of the National Notary Association because of what transpired in the early morning hours of August 3, 1923, some thirty-five years before the NNA was founded.

The dramatic scene played out at Coolidge's Vermont family farm in Plymouth Notch. Vice President Coolidge was awakened to learn of the sudden death of President Warren Harding. At around 2:30 a.m. in the living room, with his right hand placed on the family Bible, Coolidge took the Presidential oath of office by the light of a kerosene lamp. Initially, the key relevance of this event for the NNA was the fact that the oath was administered by a Vermont Notary Public, who also happened to be the new President's father, John. Subsequent artists' renderings of the scene that early morning at the Coolidge farm have become iconic, as has the story of the father awakening his son and swearing him into the world's most powerful office.

If Calvin Coolidge's only relevance for American Notaries and the National Notary Association had been the fact that he was the first and only President ever to be sworn in by a Notary Public, that might be little more than an interesting historical footnote. The more compelling connection has always been the way President Coolidge conducted his public life. And for that conduct, the NNA has long elevated Coolidge as a shining example of what a conscientious and selfless public servant should be.

Notaries, as public officers, are expected to perform their duties with integrity, evenhandedness and scrupulous attention to propriety. It is these very same personal qualities that enabled Coolidge to set his impeccable example as a public servant. But this does not comprise the sole reason that, out of all the American Presidents, Notaries may feel a special kinship to Coolidge. Our thirtieth President was above all a man of small town common sense and virtue — a modest man of no modest talents who preferred to stay in the background as he enabled others to fulfill their own talents and dreams. Notaries are drawn to Coolidge's integrity, his humility, his common touch, his love of family, his inclination to surrender the spotlight to others, and perhaps also to the fact that his role in American life, like their own, has long been underestimated and misunderstood.

Though Calvin Coolidge wielded the full powers of the American Presidency — and he did so as ably and effectively as any Chief Executive of the twentieth century — he never lost his feel for the small town nor his concern for the common man and his compassion for the underdog. He preferred the common touch to the imperial Presidency, and Americans of the day sensed this and loved him for it. This is not to say that he lacked formality. Indeed, Coolidge transformed a Harding White House whose moral tenor, according to one acute observer, was that of the backroom of a speakeasy, to a place where the people's business was conducted with propriety, integrity and due process.

Coolidge was one of those rare men who are so secure in themselves that they never worry that people will think less of them for not talking. In a garrulous era of business boosterism and of Sinclair Lewis-style "Babbittry," Coolidge seemed to be — as more than one observer has noted — the anti-Babbitt. He was as unlikely a figurehead as could be imagined for the boisterous Jazz Age. Even so, American entrepreneurs never had a better friend or booster than "Silent Cal," whose every impulse and action as President was to unfetter American business.

The purpose of this book is to acquaint new generations of Americans with the considerable virtues and achievements of a President who, if he is regarded at all beyond academic circles nowadays, is typically caricatured beyond recognition. However, dispelling caricatures is not a task that we are unfamiliar with at the NNA. Indeed, our Association for decades has had to explain to the public the critical fraud-deterrent role of the often satirized and widely misunderstood American Notary. I might point out, though, that in the wake of the horrific events of September 11, 2001, Americans seem to have a growing appreciation of the identity-screening function of the Notary, being now more than well aware that the impostors among us may have intentions more sinister and fatal than mere fraud.

We are honored that not only the nation's top Coolidge authorities and scholars responded to our call to explain "Why Coolidge Matters," but also a number of others who have dedicated their lives to public service and well know the pressures and burdens that Coolidge handled with such uncommon grace. Our panel of authors includes liberals and conservatives, academics and journalists, activists and thinkers. Their original essays, which vary markedly in length, focus and perspective, were edited only for unity of style. We chose, for example, to capitalize every mention of "President," "Presidential" and "Presidency."

The essays, which are not presented in any particular chronology, teem with anecdotes, insights and analyses about the life, career and character of this nation's thirtieth Chief Executive. Each essay — from every author — could easily stand on its own as an in-depth testament to aspects of Coolidge's life, ideals and legacy. But combined together in this volume, the essays in their entirety reveal an even more extensive and captivating picture of Calvin Coolidge.

We learn about a man with a penetrating and highly organized intellect, whose predecessor in the White House was overwhelmed by details, but who himself was in full command of these details and thus the master of every situation. We learn about a man of deep faith, whose policies brought prosperity to the nation, but whose constant message was that matters of the spirit come first. We learn about a man who championed the rights of the vulnerable — notably women, blacks and the mentally ill — long before it was politically fashionable to do so. And we learn about a man who answered not to party bosses or political dogma, but to his own conscience and common sense.

The essays puncture a number of myths about Coolidge, such as the one that he was barely verbal because he had little to say. Actually, Coolidge was one of the most communicative of all American Presidents and became a virtual media maestro as he masterfully utilized the new media of radio and film. It is estimated that during his six years in office, Coolidge held an unprecedented five-hundred twenty press conferences, which breaks down to about eight a month. One wishes that the Presidents of recent decades had been so communicative. He also wrote his own speeches. Still, there's no doubt that Coolidge highly prized silence when words were not needed and to a degree cultivated the myth of the laconic Yankee — one reason that the words he did say were so powerful.

Perhaps it was the personalized act of respect by the newly elected President Ronald Reagan that triggered the current interest in President Calvin Coolidge. Reagan, upon assuming office in January of 1981, had two portraits hung in the Cabinet Room at the White House. One was of Franklin D. Roosevelt. That might have been predicted. But the other was of Calvin Coolidge. And it raised eyebrows and questions. When asked about the portrait, Reagan said, "You hear a lot of jokes about…Coolidge, but I think the joke is on the people that make jokes…if you look at his record."

Reagan clearly thought that Coolidge still mattered. As certainly did Gerald Ford, who shared with Coolidge the similar monumental experience of healing a wounded nation that had lost faith in its leadership due to a national scandal — Watergate in the case of Ford and Teapot Dome in the case of Coolidge.

Coolidge still matters because the American Presidency today, more than ever before, is subject to a media-driven scrutiny that would be unimaginable to our

Founding Fathers. How should a President conduct himself or herself in the glaring light of such scrutiny? Well, it is hard to imagine a better model of Presidential conduct than Calvin Coolidge, nor a better motto for any occupant of the Oval Office than, "What would Coolidge do?" Is it possible to conceive, for example, a Coolidge who would idly sit by as aides discussed implementing a rancorous "wedge" campaign purposely to divide Americans rather than to unite them?

"What would Coolidge do?" You can read about it in this book.

I hope readers will share this book with others, especially with young people, who will gain a heightened respect for American democracy from our thirtieth President's unwavering commitment to service and integrity.

The Loud Silence of Calvin Coolidge

By James H. Douglas
Governor of Vermont

Vermonters cherish the idea that the place endows its residents with a special magic, bred in small town life, in small schools, and the small democracy of town meetings, sufficient to change the world, or at least to breed into its young the soul of freedom and independent thinking that can compete with those who are raised in faster-moving places. There is something about the place that embosses on those born and raised here a character, stoic, resolute, instinctively adaptable, and born of having to make do with what you have.

John Deere was born in Rutland in 1804, worked as a blacksmith until the age of thirty-three, moved to Illinois, invented and marketed the first commercially successful steel plow, and changed American farming and world farming forever. Illinois claims him as one of its own, but Vermont is loath to give up the connection. John Deere was a Vermonter, who made a success in Illinois.

George Dewey was born in Montpelier in 1837. Educated in the common schools, he left Vermont for the Naval Academy at age seventeen, quickly rose in rank, as Commodore Dewey led the force that destroyed the Spanish fleet at Manila Bay in 1898, and became a national hero. He made his mark outside Vermont, but he is another of the select group of expatriates who will always be Vermonters, even though they left their mark on the world, far beyond the sanctuary of the Green Mountains.

Vermont celebrates two Presidents of the United States as native sons. The first was Chester A. Arthur, born in Fairfield in 1829, raised in his father's school in Williston, who attended Union College in Schenectady, then moved to New York City and a law practice, then politics, Vice President, and then President by virtue of the death of James A. Garfield. The other is Calvin Coolidge.

Calvin Coolidge was born in Plymouth Notch in 1872, was raised and educated there until he left for Amherst College in 1891, then became a lawyer in Northampton, its mayor, a State Representative, State Senator, Massachusetts Lieutenant Governor, Governor, Vice President, and President upon the death of Warren Harding. He won the office in 1924, retired in 1929, and died four years later. He was, and will always be remembered as a Vermonter or, more directly, *the* Vermonter.

What does that mean? It means he was a quiet, conservative, careful man whose first experiences colored everything he did after he left Plymouth Notch. Massachusetts may try to claim him, but he is ours, once and forever a Vermonter.

Edward G. Lowry published *Washington Close-Ups* in 1921, subtitled "Intimate Views of Some Public Figures." Of Coolidge, then Vice President, he wrote, in spite of his efforts, Coolidge "has revealed nothing, disclosed nothing." At Washington dinner parties, he stood "quite still, and saying not a blessed word, though all about him were babble and laughter and conversation. He didn't seem ill at ease or embarrassed or tongue-tied. He was just still." Lowry called him the "foster-child of silence."

When news of Warren Harding's unexpected passing arrived in Plymouth Notch, the night of August 3, 1923, his father, a Vermont Notary Public, administered the oath of office to his son. It was 2:30 in the morning. After the ceremony, everyone went back to bed.

There it is, right there. Everyone went back to bed. It was the middle of the night, when good people were supposed to be asleep. That act put the Presidency in its place. The next morning everything would change, but, after the swearing in, they resumed their rest. That the new President could go to sleep reveals his self-possession and his character.

Not everyone who qualifies as a Vermonter is like that. Yankee Doodle, with a feather in his cap, the rube, the hayseed, with candor and a wit, is and always was a stereotype. Brother Jonathan, in Royall Tyler's 1787 play "The Contrast," is the first literary example of this, but it was a classic type long before that date. Jonathan spoke plainly, from the heart. He was unsophisticated in the city, but the lessons he learned at home made him superior to the decadence of urban life in all respects.

For the ages, without taking anything away from Ethan Allen and George Aiken, Calvin Coolidge is the most famous of Vermonters. He stands for all the values Vermonters cherish. Even as the state grows more "progressive," Coolidge remains a model of the Vermont character — an anchor in the mainstream.

They made great fun of him. At the theater one evening, Groucho Marx stepped out of the traditional mayhem of his brothers' performance to the edge of the stage, looked up at the Presidential box and asked, "Isn't it past your bedtime, Mr. President?" Alice Roosevelt Longworth said he looked like he had been weaned on a pickle. Dorothy Parker, informed of his death, asked, "How could they tell?"

Coolidge played to the caricature. He put on an Indian headdress while visiting South Dakota, and was photographed in a variety of getups, all of it in good humor and with that famous dour, inscrutable face, showing no emotion. On that trip he said, "I do not choose to run for President in 1928." The economy of that statement was pure Coolidge, as was its disavowal of ambition.

He turned down a second term. After Hoover's inauguration, he walked out of the White House and went home, a private citizen, demonstrating to everyone what was important to him. He had served his country, and he was content with that. There was no need to do more.

Will Rogers said of Coolidge, "He doesn't say much, but when he does say something, he don't say much." Coolidge himself explained his theory of silence, although nailing down precisely what he did say on that subject is difficult. One biographer reported that he said, "I don't recall any candidate for President that ever injured himself by not talking." Another quoted Coolidge saying, "If you don't say anything you won't have to repeat it." Another version goes, "They can't hang you for what you don't say." Most familiar is the version that goes, "What you don't say can't hurt you." Maybe Calvin Coolidge said all of these things. Maybe what he actually said was blander, and history has jazzed it up, but the point is made.

Silence is a form of expression. We don't have nearly enough of it these days. Everybody has something to say, and few seem to keep it to themselves. Television and radio and blogs on the net are so much babble, I sometimes wish our culture could be weaned on a Coolidge.

Once he said, "No one ever listened themselves out of a job." That is as interesting as the "don't say" quote. The silence of Silent Cal was not inactive or somnolent. It was a way of thinking and working out problems. It was selfless. The ego didn't intrude on the issue. The person was not the job. The self didn't fill the room with its own importance, strangling all discussion. You listened first, and then you listened some more. When you spoke, it was because you had something to say. Otherwise, you said nothing.

The national historic site that is Calvin Coolidge's birthplace in Plymouth is a sacred place for all who visit it. It is a place where time seems to have stopped. The house, and particularly the parlor where John Coolidge administered the oath of office to his son Calvin, holding the family Bible in his hands, has been restored as if it were 1923 and the ceremony had just concluded. Down the road, two marble stones mark the final resting place of the thirtieth President of the United States and Grace Goodhue Coolidge, his loving wife.

Calvin Coolidge returned to Vermont many times after he left, and then he returned for good, to join the others who had gone into that ground, lying "pillowed on the loving breast of our everlasting hills." That is part of the quote that appears on the walls of the Vermont State House, and is read by every visitor to the Capitol. It is read by the legislators who return to that building every January, and by this Governor, regularly. It ends as a prayer: "If the spirit of liberty should vanish in other parts of the union and support of our institutions should languish, it could all be replenished from the generous store held by the people of this brave little state of Vermont."

He spoke those words in 1928, while on a visit to the state to see, for himself, the damage caused by the 1927 flood. Those words inspired Vermonters then, and continue to do so today. They were the words of a man known for his silence, and they sound all the more moving because of that.

Coolidge has been called the luckiest President, for not taking that second term and not being blamed for the Depression and the stock market crash of 1929. His years as President were calm and peaceful and prosperous. People were proud to be Americans. We weren't at war. A small town President was just what was needed, as an antidote to the roar of the Twenties.

Calvin Coolidge stands out as a real person who happened to become President. Line him up with Ronald Reagan, the Roosevelts, John Kennedy, Jefferson, Lincoln and Washington, and he seems to be a lesser President.

There are no Calvin Coolidges on the national political stage today. Quiet doesn't muster votes. It is a different time. Still, we would be lucky to have leaders who understand the Coolidge idea, who don't have all the answers, who understand how to listen, who keep some opinions private, who are unwilling to become a public spectacle, who are humble and patient and thoughtful. We need leaders who serve because they have something to give, and not because they want to hold the office.

Every one of us could use a little Coolidge now and again. We could all afford to be just a little less ambitious, a little less the center of the world, a little less wordy. We could practice silence as a restorative experience. We could waste less. We could save more. We could be more careful. We could live simpler lives.

He was what the country needed at the time. When we are very lucky, we get what we need; usually, we get what we deserve. That's a puritanical idea, and Coolidge was one of the last of that species of quiet, serious pilgrims. William Allen White entitled his 1938 biography of Calvin Coolidge, "A Puritan in Babylon." Coolidge, of all the Presidents, is simplicity personified.

That idea is conservative in nature. It says we should try to improve what we have, to make it work, rather than throwing out tradition and trying something new. It finds virtue in direct talk and direct action. It is cautious and careful. It says "no" more often than "yes," and it is principled. It recognizes the value of experience, and the risk of overreaching. It is steady and forthright and quiet. It recognizes that public service is a trust, not a podium or a pulpit.

Calvin Coolidge is the inspiration for the young who yearn to be President someday. He is gone now, but he is still here, as an idea.

At the White House, circa 1925.

Famous sculptor Henry K. Bush-Brown works on his bas-relief portrait of Calvin Coolidge, March 5, 1925.

HIS LEGACY IS A MODEL

By M. Jodi Rell

"We all need to step back and create a different perspective on what it means to serve the public, and on what we desire from our elected officials: leadership and ideas."

The world and the United States have changed dramatically since the early decades of the twentieth century. But in many ways, the world is very much the same. The problems, on their face, appear to be different, but at their core lie the same issues that have existed for years. More than ever, the world demands strong leaders with the courage to make difficult decisions, while possessing the compassion to deal with the frailties of the human condition.

One of the most endearing qualities of a leader is consistency. People want to know where you stand on things — they want to believe that you are not going to renege on decisions when the pressure increases. They want to trust you and believe in you. These virtues in a leader still ring true today, possibly more than ever.

Trust and consistency in carrying out the responsibilities of this country's highest office — the President of the United States — were dutifully embodied by the nation's thirtieth President, Calvin Coolidge.

When we examine U.S. Presidents, past and present, Calvin Coolidge is often overlooked. If he is mentioned in history or civics classes in high school, it is usually

Attending a meeting of the National Academy of Science and Research Council, April 28, 1924.

a reference as to how he came to be President with the passing of Warren G. Harding. Even in New England, where he lived all of his life besides his time in Washington, D.C., as Vice President and President, he rarely receives his just due.

Why? Because many Presidents are more demonstrative, or the times during which they served have their own historical significance, such as wars or a depression, or they are embroiled in scandal. We tend not to remember the ones that focus on the business of leading this nation with little fanfare and a steady hand. Calvin Coolidge was certainly one of those Presidents.

As we look back at his tenure in office, President Coolidge is not remembered for building a canal or landing a man on the moon. Rather, he took more of a practical approach to governing — he helped government run efficiently and empowered communities and businesses to support themselves and flourish, which built a stronger nation. During his tenure in the White House the country and the world were emerging from tumultuous times. The First World War had recently ended, and memories of one of the worst influenza pandemics in centuries were still fresh on everyone's consciousness.

Instead of having the government be all things to all people, President Coolidge recognized that it was more important to be open and honest with the people and not pretend to be something he was not. While certainly a man of few words, he clearly understood human nature and his approach is as right today as it was during his tenure.

He knew what it was like to live and work in a small town. He had gained incredible and insightful experience serving at the local level. That experience in Northhampton, Massachusetts, provided him with a real understanding as to how government worked, as well as where it came up short. It also demonstrated to him how important it was to be yourself as a politician. The people in your hometown oftentimes know you better than you know yourself.

The perspective he gained from being involved in local politics is a critical one to have when governing, especially today. In many ways, we are less connected to each other than ever before, and that is a direct result of being more connected in other ways. Today's world is a blur compared to the 1920's. The Earth is not spinning any faster on its axis; rather, technology has evolved to such a degree that it only takes a split second for information to travel around the globe. One of the unfortunate by-products of the ever-faster exchange of information is the growing sense that we are losing touch with the community in which we live.

The Internet and other technological advances have created an atmosphere in which we never again have to walk into the lobby of a bank, buy a newspaper at a news stand or visit the local branch of our library. As a result, we have lost touch with our neighbors, our community and many of our politicians. We may know more about a wider variety of things, but we are starting to know less about the important things occurring around us every day.

Would this significant advancement in technology and information sharing alter the approach of President Coolidge? Absolutely not. In many ways, he was ahead of his time — quite skilled and adept at using the technology of his day to connect with the public. He was the first President to deliver a speech to the entire nation over the radio. He was also the first President to appear on film with sound. President Coolidge was not a celebrity by any stretch. However, he used the technology available to him at that time to forge a better connection with the public, not to peddle his ideas and shape his image.

President Coolidge did not do things just to do things — he did things with a purpose and for a purpose. He was criticized during his tenure for not traveling down to the Gulf States following the Great Mississippi Flood and touring the destruction. Instead, he spent his time in Washington working on plans to help those who needed assistance following the storm, passing up the photo opportunity for real governing.

During his life as a public servant, Coolidge faced a number of crises. No matter the situation or challenge, he was decisive and consistent. While

With Herbert Hoover and members of the Radioman Association, October 7, 1924.

Governor of the Commonwealth of Massachusetts, Coolidge was confronted with the Boston Police Strike. Initially, he left it to the principal parties involved to work things out. However, as the situation escalated into a public safety situation with the City on the verge of riots, Governor Coolidge stepped in swiftly and decisively to immediately ensure that the public was protected. He did not waver or blink throughout the crisis, no matter how much pressure was brought to bear on him by the clashing sides.

As we look at the present political landscape and reflect back on Coolidge's approach during both quiet and difficult times, one cannot help but appreciate his even hand and decisiveness. It is hard to truly find those qualities in many of our present leaders — individuals who can stand in the face of blistering pressure — and stay committed to an idea, a proposal, or a plan that they believe is in the collective best interest of the public. It was not that he was stubborn; rather, he gave each and every decision very careful consideration and, when he made a decision, he was apt to stick with it.

As leaders, we should all embody this approach because we are elected to serve the public — not to be swayed by grandstanding or to vacillate while making decisions. As I look back on Coolidge's Presidency, I cannot help but admire how he comported himself throughout his time in the White House. People often confuse Coolidge's approach as lacking compassion or as indifference. He was neither.

He cared very deeply about the people he was elected to serve — possibly more than any other President. He always put the public first and foremost when weighing decisions. He viewed government as a body to help manage affairs and set a course for the nation to help it grow and prosper.

In many ways, Coolidge was a progressive leader — allowing the country to run its course with his steady influence while championing efforts and causes others had overlooked, including the care of veterans and women's suffrage. Understanding the inter-workings of local, state and federal government, he allowed those closest to the pulse of their community to continue to make policy for the people they served, without interference from the federal government.

President Coolidge's experience at the local level also taught him another valuable lesson — treat everyone fairly and never malign your opponent. Oftentimes, your opponent in a local election is someone you know — somebody who is part of your community. Calvin Coolidge did not speak ill of his opponents and try to raise up his prospects as a candidate by bringing his opponent down. He ran on the issues and wanted the electorate to choose their leaders based on ideas and principles. We could all learn from this approach. The public wants to make educated and knowledgeable decisions when choosing their elected officials. Unfortunately, these days, policies, ideas and platforms take a back seat to personal attacks and mudslinging. We all need to step back and create a different perspective on what it means to serve the public, and on what we desire from our elected officials: leadership and ideas, not rhetoric and aspersions.

Nearly eighty years have passed since Calvin Coolidge served as this country's thirtieth President. And while the world has changed, the qualities we look for in our leaders remain very much the same. We want our leaders to be trustworthy and open. We want them to be consistent and compassionate. We want them to guide our country forward, allowing the public to dream, experience and grow. And we want to be proud of them. Calvin Coolidge embodied all of these ideals.

As the Governor of the great state of Connecticut, I strive to emulate Coolidge's abilities to lead and govern. Connecticut is often referred to as the "Land of Steady Habits," and, although he spent most of his life in the neighboring state of Massachusetts, Coolidge was a man who would have felt right at home in Connecticut with his steady and consistent approach. His legacy serves as model for all of us today, regardless of the positions we hold in our communities. To help this country continue to move forward, we should all emulate Coolidge and let his legacy shape how we approach the incredible responsibilities bestowed upon us by the people we serve.

M. Jodi Rell is Connecticut's 87th Governor and the state's first-ever woman Republican chief executive. She's held elected office in Connecticut for more than two decades. She served as the 105th Lieutenant Governor for over nine years, and represented the 107th District of Brookfield in the state House of Representatives. In 2003, she was named a Melvin Jones Fellow, the highest form of recognition conferred by the Lions Club International Foundation for representing humanitarian qualities such as generosity, compassion and concern for the less fortunate.

Decoration Day at Arlington National Cemetery, May 30, 1925.

THE INFLUENTIAL ORATOR

By Robert H. Ferrell

"That Coolidge had an effect, even beyond whatever political messages he desired to impart, and managed to do it in fine fashion, is undeniable."

An American's casual impression of President Coolidge as a speaker is that he was a dry, uninteresting individual who, among other defects, could not make a speech that anyone wished to hear. I remember a wall in Forbes Library, the public library of Northampton, Massachusetts, where Grace Coolidge arranged for a collection of family photographs and memorabilia, among which was a sort of speaking tube. On the wall below was a button, and in those antediluvian days before buttons were commonplace in museums this button held its attraction. So, I would press it to hear a short recording of some Coolidge speech of the 1920s. The President of those times apparently was speaking through his nose. "Alpha and omega," went the first part of the speech, the phrase applicable to some important point of the 1920s. In imitating the speech to students in my classes, I would hold my nose and sound exactly like Coolidge.

Of course I took no interest in the sound reproduction problems of the 1920s, which included the lack of overtones in the rolls or records, whatever the medium — perhaps a hand-cranked Victrola — of the time. The squeaky production at the

At the memorial service held in honor of President George Washington's 190th birthday.

library always reminded me of one of the smart remarks made about Coolidge somewhat earlier, when he was Lieutenant Governor of Massachusetts and Samuel W. McCall Governor. It was said that the latter, a skilled orator, could fill any hall and Coolidge could empty it.

To my students I attributed Coolidge's lack of oratorical skill to his not trying very hard. He had a well-known habit of never doing anything politically that someone else could do for him, and I calculated that he let McCall do the work.

When he became Vice President and President in the 1920s, there was another reason he did not need to try to speak forcefully, and this was the appearance of loudspeakers. President Woodrow Wilson was first to experience the mechanism that would change American oratory. In the earlier era of Daniel Webster, Henry Clay and John C. Calhoun, orators had to shout so their voices would reach the fringes of crowds. Wilson, an old-fashioned orator since the 1880s, was accustomed to shouting, and first encountered loudspeakers in San Diego in 1919. Because he could not move around easily and had to remain close to the microphone, he did not like them.

The truth — I did not know it — was that Coolidge in the 1920s gave large attention to his speeches, whatever his practice before that. And he was very effective, especially with the new medium of radio, which "came in" at the same time as loudspeakers. A few years later it became even easier for listeners to understand because of the commercial sets turned out by manufacturers, rather than of the earlier handmade sets. Coolidge's voice, admittedly a little nasal (if one can judge from recordings, ignoring their defects), came over the radio clearly. It was distinct. It was an attractive voice. The President pronounced words with a New England accent; it was said that he could pronounce the word *cow* in four syllables. Whatever the accent, people liked what they heard. It perhaps persuaded Middle Westerners and other auditors that the President was especially cultivated — he had attended Amherst College, the well-known Eastern institution. They could hear it well, despite the tangle of wires that covered frames at the tops of their radio sets.

Apart from the sheer clarity that Coolidge could offer, there was the care with which the President prepared his addresses. He was one of the last presidents to write his own speeches. His successor Herbert Hoover seems to have written most of his speeches, though Hoover's talks were hardly inspiring and critics attributed them, fact-laden and wordy as they were, to his personality, that of a mining engineer ("the great engineer") who had taken up politics. But Coolidge, a professional politician, wrote his own speeches and labored over them with intensity. His wife knew when he was doing a speech, for he would turn irritable and sharp with the two Coolidge sons, snapping at them for almost any reason. He secreted himself in the old West Wing office put up in the time of Theodore Roosevelt, before the 1929 fire destroyed it to make way for the present West Wing with its oval office, and dictated his speeches to a secretary who typed them triple space, whereupon the President with his black-ink pen would go over them, changing this or that word. Coolidge's speech drafts are in Northampton's Forbes Library today for anyone to see first-hand the pains with which Presidential addresses were written in the 1920s.

The result of the very clear Coolidge delivery, and the intense care with which Coolidge wrote out his ideas, was a huge collection of speeches. Frankly, it was surprising how many of these carefully carpentered speeches Coolidge gave. They almost blanketed the oratorical scene in 1923-29 and set Coolidge far ahead of other contemporary political leaders. When he was Vice President, he did not get a chance to show

Speaking at the cornerstone laying on the future site of the Jewish Community Center, May 3, 1925.

his oratorical skills. President Warren G. Harding sent Coolidge out to give speeches in small places, such as an address in Canton, Ohio, in memory of President William McKinley. But beginning in August, 1923, the nation was eager to know something about the hitherto silent man who had been Vice President. His voice supplied the information people desired.

That Coolidge had an effect, even beyond whatever messages he desired to impart, and managed to do it in fine fashion, is undeniable. The late Rear Admiral Eugene R. Fluckey, who grew up in the 1920s, constantly credited the speeches of President Coolidge as the influence and inspiration upon his event-starred life. It is moving testimony indeed to the greatness of the thirtieth President from the person I consider the best U.S. Navy submarine commander in World War II.

Robert H. Ferrell Ph. D., retired from the faculty of Indiana University, is an expert on American foreign policy and the history of the U.S. Presidency. He is the author of *The Presidency of Calvin Coolidge; American Diplomacy: The Twentieth Century; Harry S. Truman: A Life; Presidential Leadership: From Woodrow Wilson to Harry S. Truman,* and *Grace Coolidge: The People's Lady in Silent Cal's White House.*

Addressing a congregation at Arlington National Cemetery, circa 1924.

Major League baseball player and manager of the Washington Senators Stanley Raymond "Bucky" Harris presents Coolidge with the baseball used to open the 1924 World Series.

AN ENABLER OF PROSPERITY

BY BURTON FOLSOM, JR.

"Coolidge, we must always remember, wanted prosperity as a means, not an end."

Why Calvin Coolidge matters, first, is because limited government worked well during his Presidency — an ideal that is not tried often enough today. Second, Coolidge had strong character, which reflected his loyalty to principles of freedom and constitutional government. Let me explore these two themes in more detail.

Coolidge came to political maturity in the Progressive Era (1900-1920). During these years, the "progressive spirit" led many politicians to argue that a stronger central government was needed to solve the economic problems of the day. Coolidge resisted this trend and argued that adherence to the Constitution and the principles of the Declaration of Independence well served the nation before the 1900s, and would continue to do so afterward.

The Declaration of Independence reflected a generation of thinking on the subject of natural rights — "that all men are created equal, that they are endowed by their Creator with certain unalienable rights, that among these are life, liberty, and the pursuit of happiness." Government was not the source of

Attending the circus, circa 1924

rights; God was. In fact, government to the Founders was a potential source of tyranny, and the Constitution that was written eleven years later separated the powers of government in order to protect life, liberty and property from future encroachments by potential tyrants.

Certainly, in the view of the Founders, people might abuse freedom, but that problem was much more easily addressed than that of leaders with power abusing that power. The historic pattern, the Founders argued, was for man, when given power, to oppress and even enslave his fellow men. The antidote was limited government. According to James Madison, "In framing a government which is to be administered by men over men, the great difficulty lies in this: You must first enable the government to control the governed; and in the next place oblige it to control itself." Coolidge accepted Madison's conclusion, but most progressives did not.

The views of Coolidge on the Founders contrast sharply with those of President Woodrow Wilson. Wilson, a progressive President, had little use for the Founders and the Declaration. "If you want to understand the real Declaration of Independence," Wilson urged, "do not read the preface." Government did not exist merely to protect rights. Instead, Wilson argued that the Declaration "expressly leaves to each generation of men the determination of what they will do with their lives ... In brief, political liberty is the right of those who are governed to adjust the government to their own needs and interests."

"We are not," Wilson insisted, "bound to adhere to the doctrines held by the signers of the Declaration of Independence."

The limited government enshrined in both the Declaration and the Constitution may have been an advance for the Founders, Wilson conceded, but society had evolved since then. The modern state of the early 1900s was "beneficent" and "indispensable." Separation of powers hindered modern governments from promoting progress. "The only fruit of dividing power," Wilson asserted, "was to make it irresponsible."

A better "constitutional government," Wilson urged, was one "whose powers have been adapted to the interests of its people." A strong executive was needed, he believed, to translate the interests of the people into public policy. The President was the opinion leader, the "spokesman for the real sentiment and purpose of the country." And what the country needed was "a man who will be and who will seem to the country in some sort of an embodiment of the character and purpose it wishes its government to have — a man who understood his own day and the needs of his country."

In the White House, Wilson became a strong President working with a "living Constitution." He promoted the expanding of "beneficent" government into new areas. In his second year as President, he concluded that shipping rates were too high, and he blessed his Secretary of Treasury's plan to regulate overseas shipping rates and the companies doing the shipping. Later he promoted a plan to make loans to farmers at federally subsidized rates. Then he pushed through Congress a bill fixing an eight-hour day for railroad workers.

Article I, Section 8, of the Constitution gives no power to the federal government to regulate the prices of trade, the hours of work, or to make special loans to farmers or any other group. But Wilson said he was operating with a "living Constitution" and that increased government in these cases reflected appropriately the greater will of the people. Likewise, when Wilson helped centralize banking with the Federal Reserve banking system and when he further restricted trade by promoting the Clayton Antitrust Act, he believed that this work for the general good outweighed any loyalties to the rigid construction set up by the Founders in the original Constitution.

Such growth of government came with a cost, but Wilson was ready with the progressive income tax to pay for his new programs. World War I clearly influenced Wilson's use of the tax and his centralization of power — he promoted an increase in the top tax rate from seven to fifteen percent in 1916; then, during the war, Wilson secured an increase to a seventy-seven percent marginal rate on the country's largest incomes.

Where Wilson supported an evolving Constitution that gave him authority to increase the power of government and centralize power, President Calvin Coolidge, who was on the ticket that succeeded Wilson, believed that the Declaration and the Constitution should be accepted as the Founders wrote them.

In July 1926, on the sesquicentennial of the signing of the Declaration, Coolidge gave a speech reaffirming the need for limited government. "It is not so much then for the purpose of undertaking to proclaim new theories and principles that this annual celebration is maintained, but rather to reaffirm and reestablish those old theories and principles which time and the unerring logic of events have demonstrated to be sound."

Coolidge added that "there is a finality" about the Declaration. "If all men are created equal, that is final. If they are endowed with inalienable rights, that is final. If governments derive their just powers from the consent of the governed, that is final. No advance, no progress can be made beyond these propositions. If anyone wishes to deny their truth or their soundness, the only direction in which he can proceed historically is not forward, but backward toward the time when there was no equality, no rights of the individual, no rule of the people. Those who wish to proceed in that direction can not lay claim to progress. They are reactionary. Their ideas are not more modern, but more ancient, than those of the Revolutionary fathers."

Coolidge's attitude as President reflected his belief in the ideas of the Declaration. He was not always consistent — for example, he signed the Fordney-McCumber Tariff in 1922, which slapped high and uneven taxes on some very needed imports. But his efforts were largely in the direction of reducing the size of government to increase liberty. For example, Coolidge cut the size of government and was the last President to have budget surpluses every year of his Presidency. Also, when the Harding-Coolidge administration came into office in 1921, the tax rate on top incomes was seventy-three percent; when Coolidge left the presidency eight years later, it was twenty-five percent. The rates on the lowest incomes were also slashed. Finally, he also helped eliminate or reduce excise taxes, which hit poorer groups in society more heavily than the rich.

Coolidge often attacked special interests. He vetoed a bill to give a special cash bonus to veterans; and, through President Harding, he was part of the administration that shut down a government-operated steel plant set up by President Wilson, but which had lost money each year of its operation.

Coolidge always believed that if government were expanded beyond its constitutional limits — as Wilson wanted to do — the result of the progressives' good intentions would be more lobbying and more special-interest pleading. In fact, he viewed the President as the bulwark against subsidies for politically shrewd lobbies. "It is because in their hours of timidity the Congress becomes subservient to the importunities of organized minorities that the President comes more and more to stand as the champion of the rights of the whole country," Coolidge observed. "Organizing such minorities has come to be a well-recognized industry at Washington. They are oftentimes led by persons of great ability, who display much skill in bringing their influences to bear on the Congress."

One of the most powerful of these lobbies were the farmers. Under Article I, Section 8, of the Constitution, the Founders permitted no aid to farmers or any other group. Wilson, however, had increased federal support — usually in the form of loans — to farmers, and many farm organizations were anxious to argue for direct federal aid to support the prices of crops.

Not once, but twice Coolidge courageously vetoed the McNary-Haugen farm bill, which was popular with farmers because it promised federal price supports for them. Coolidge looked beyond the good intentions of the bill to the potential harm that would be done by expanding the power of government. "This legislation proposes, in effect, that Congress shall delegate to a Federal Farm Board, nominated by farmers, the power to fix and collect a tax, called an equalization fee, on certain products produced by those farmers. That certainly contemplates a

With newspaper correspondents on the White House South Lawn, circa 1923.

remarkable delegation of the taxing power … This so-called equalization fee … is a tax for the special benefit of particular groups."

If enacted, Coolidge realized, the McNary-Haugen bill would be a precedent for other groups to secure subsidies for their occupations, all at the expense of taxpayers in general. High taxes would then stifle American industry and reduce incentives for Americans to go into business. The American edge in world trade, created in Coolidge's view by the freedom given under the Constitution, would be removed and the American standard of living would decline.

"I do not believe," Coolidge wrote in his veto of McNary-Haugen, "that upon serious consideration the farmers of American would tolerate the precedent of a body of men chosen solely by one industry who, acting in the name of the government, shall arrange for contracts which determine prices, secure the buying and selling of commodities, the levying of taxes on that industry, and pay losses on foreign dumping of any surplus." Furthermore, "The granting of any such arbitrary power to a Government board is to run counter to our traditions, the philosophy of our Government, the spirit of our institutions, and all principles of equity."

If we evaluate Coolidge's views by the economic results of his six years in the White House, we must judge him a success. Unemployment averaged three-point-three per cent and inflation only one percent during his Presidency. Economists lump unemployment and inflation together and label it "the misery index." Coolidge's misery index of four-point-three percent is the lowest of any President in the twentieth century. Furthermore, under Coolidge per capita income jumped, and the national debt was slashed during each of his six years as President.

Coolidge, we must always remember, wanted prosperity as a means, not an end. True, he said, "the chief business of the American people is business," but he said later in that speech, "Of course, the accumulation of wealth cannot be justified as the chief end of existence…. The power of the spirit always prevails over the power of the flesh." Wealth was a means, Coolidge argued, to "many other things that we want very much more. We want peace and honor, and that charity which is so strong an element of all civilization. The chief ideal of the American people is idealism."

Coolidge tied the creation of wealth and the enjoyment of spiritual things to a strong Constitution and the principles of the Declaration. In that speech in 1926, on the one-hundred fiftieth anniversary of the signing of the Declaration, Coolidge argued that the document itself "is the product of the spiritual insight of the people. We live in an age of science and of abounding accumulation of material things. These did not create our Declaration. Our Declaration created them. The things of the spirit come first." Coolidge concluded, "Unless we cling to that, all our material prosperity, overwhelming though it may appear, will turn to a barren scepter in our grasp. If we are to maintain the great heritage which has been bequeathed to us, we must be like-minded as the fathers who created it. We must not sink into a pagan materialism. We must cultivate the reverence which they had for the things that are holy. We must follow the spiritual and moral leadership which they showed."

Coolidge's view of freedom and limited government clearly shaped his conception of the Presidency. Granted, he was a taciturn man, not given to showy public displays. But part of this reticence reflects his idea that the presidency is not really where the action should be. The Founders placed the responsibility for the success of the country in the hands of Americans themselves. Government was limited so that people could build the country and live free lives. Their success, not that of a President, would determine the national fate and the national character.

Sometimes Coolidge's playful actions as President reflected his view that free people, more than an activist President, were the real source of the nation's accomplishments. When he had to shake hands with large groups of people, as he often did, he liked to move quickly through the line — perhaps in part to avoid having to respond to requests for subsidies. Also, rapidly moving through the line was his implicit statement that what he was doing was not as important as what others outside were doing to develop the resources of the nation. In his autobiography, Coolidge proudly writes, "On one occasion I shook hands with nineteen-hundred (people) in thirty-four minutes, which is probably my record."

Coolidge obviously did not always take himself seriously, but he always took his responsibilities for moral leadership very seriously. "The words of the

President have an enormous weight and ought not to be used indiscriminately," Coolidge warned. "There is only one form of political strategy in which I have any confidence, and that is to try to do the right thing and sometimes be able to succeed." To Coolidge, that meant that ethics were not relative, but absolute. Obeying the Constitution, and submitting to its limiting powers, was not just a duty for the President, but was a moral necessity.

Coolidge traced his views on moral absolutes to his family and to his favorite professor, Charles Garman at Amherst College. "In ethics," Coolidge said, Garman "taught us that there is a standard of righteousness, that might does not make right, that the end does not justify the means and that expediency as a working principle is bound to fail." Coolidge matters because these ideas need to be presented and defended today to preserve the economic and spiritual heritage that has made America unique.

Burton Folsom, Jr., is the Charles Kline Professor of History and Management at Hillsdale College in Michigan, where he specializes in the history of the American Presidency. He received his Ph.D. in history from the University of Pittsburgh and is the author of *Urban Capitalists, Empire Builders* and *The Myth of the Robber Barons*. His latest book, *New Deal or Raw Deal?: How FDR's Economic Legacy Has Damaged America*, was published in the fall of 2008.

With Mrs. Coolidge and sons John (left), and Calvin Jr. at Plymouth Notch (undated).

Signing the Cameron Bill, which authorized the construction of the Coolidge Dam in Arizona, June 7, 1924

THE GREAT
REFRAINER

By Amity Shlaes

"Coolidge's commitment to low taxes came out of his concept of property rights. He viewed heavy taxation as the legalization of expropriation."

Many histories convey Coolidge as inactive. The suggestion is that he was weak, but to me he always seemed like a windsurfer. Even in the face of the strongest winds, he managed to hold still, or pull in. That which he did looked like no work at all, but actually took great strength. And nowhere did Coolidge demonstrate such strength more than on the waters of economics. The course he charted there gave the nation a decade of prosperity.

Consider the record. When Coolidge became President, one of his great goals was to refrain from intervening in the economy. "If you see ten troubles coming down the road, you can be sure that nine will roll into the ditch before they reach you and you have to battle with only one of them," was the Coolidge rule. Even then the country exerted enormous pressure on the Executive to "do something." But Coolidge was the great refrainer. He even withdrew the government from people's lives, when possible.

Taxation was the area where he held back, to the greatest effect. In the early 1920s, when Coolidge came into the picture as Vice President, the nation was just

Parade Grand Marshalls, undated.

completing its first great experiment with the income tax. The tax had started out as a small thing. The top rate, applicable to only to the highest earners, millionaires in today's dollars, was seven percent. Woodrow Wilson pushed that rate up dramatically, all the way to seventy-seven percent. In Wilson's time, even those at the bottom of the tax schedule paid six percent, a rate formerly reserved for the very topmost of earners. After World War I, a new Treasury Secretary, Andrew Mellon, and his President, Warren Harding, cut the top rate back down into the fifties or forties. But when Harding died suddenly in 1923, taxes were still high.

To launch a great policy, a President needs a great ally in the cabinet. Coolidge made Mellon his. One of Coolidge's first moves was to keep Mellon on. When Mellon attempted to resign, Coolidge told him, "Forget it." The hyperactive Herbert Hoover, then Commerce Secretary, irritated Coolidge, who called him "wonder boy." But Mellon, another windsurfer, pleased Coolidge. It was said that the two taciturn men conversed in pauses. Mellon became the navigator who charted Coolidge's economic course.

Their work began with the question of tax brackets. Both men disliked the fact that under Wilson, the tax schedule had gone from seven rates to dozens of rates. That system so confused the taxpayer that he didn't know what he was paying. Coolidge and Mellon viewed the multiple brackets as poor civics. They therefore drastically reduced the number of brackets, so that every man knew what he paid. Both men disliked tax-protected municipal bonds, viewing them as a shadowy dodge. But they couldn't get Congress to go along with abolition.

Their grandest work involved tax rates. Coolidge and Mellon slashed rates multiple times, eventually getting the top rate down to twenty-five per cent, a level never seen since. Mellon argued that lower rates could actually bring in great revenues because they removed disincentives to work. The Treasury could pull in the most cash if it operated like a railroad charging that price that "the traffic will bear." Coolidge put it a different way. In a 1925 speech before the Chamber of Commerce of the State of New York, he said, "When government comes unduly under the influence of business, the tendency is to develop an administration which closes the door of opportunity."

Coolidge's commitment to low taxes came out of his concept of property rights. He viewed heavy taxation as the legalization of expropriation. "I want taxes to be less that the people may have more," Coolidge once said. In fact, Coolidge disapproved of any government intervention that would erode that contract bond. He felt that, by protecting property, he was protecting not only the rich but also the rest, including those who would be wealthy in the future. "It is not property, but the right to hold property, both great and small, that our Constitution guaranteed," he said.

There was a final area where Coolidge and Mellon did much — one that also had to do with property. That was the area of monetary policy. Coolidge believed, accurately, that inflation was the twin of tax and that it, too, was expropriation. In an inflationary environment, those who held dollars would find they could buy less. This meant he was content with the tight monetary policy that Mellon pursued (in those days the Treasury had more say about monetary policy). As a result, the Twenties is one of the few decades for which the measure of "real" Gross Domestic Product is higher than that of nominal Gross Domestic Product. Lately, the relationship has been the reverse.

To be sure, there were parts of government that grew in the Coolidge

Memorial service for Warren G. Harding in the House of Representatives. Circa 1924.

years: ground for the Bureau of Internal Revenue, as the Internal Revenue Service was then called, was broken in 1927 under Coolidge's and Mellon's watch. And there were areas of economics where Coolidge steered us wrong. The Republican Party in those days was the party of the tariff. Tariffs were even written into party platforms. Coolidge, like many in the GOP, failed to recognize that tariffs hurt both the United States and its partners. Tariffs in the United States made it harder for Europe to recover from World War I — especially Germany, which struggled under an enormous load of war debt. Trade was one of those rare areas where Coolidge seemed provincial, too much the New England man. He thought "tariff stability," as he called it, was sufficient. Though the Dawes Plan to help Germany with its debt was developed in his era, Coolidge did not favor debt forgiveness. Of the European governments, he said, "They hired the money, didn't they?" He failed to understand the consequences for the United States of a Europe in despair.

But overall the President and his partner at the Treasury achieved much. The U.S. budget ran a surplus every year. The standard of living in the United States improved dramatically — electricity and autos became part of middle-class life. The economy grew at an average three and seven-tenths percentage rate annually, higher than in many other periods.

Surely Coolidge and Mellon recognized their own achievement. In 1927, *Time* magazine reported, Coolidge paid a call at the Mellon mansion in Pittsburgh and "walked near the smoky fork of the Allegheny & Monongahela Rivers." Together, the men looked at the spot on the Allegheny where George Washington fell off a raft into freezing waters. The pair probably understood that they'd avoided a few disasters of their own through their partnership.

At the end of his life, Coolidge sometimes portrayed himself as a man behind his times of yesterday. After his Presidency, he wrote that "when I read of these newfangled things that are now so popular I realize that my time in public affairs is past." His decade, the 1920s, looked like a bubbly aberration during the dark and earnest Depression days.

In fact, however, it was the 1930s that proved the aberration — the century that followed Coolidge was one of continued growth. Some of that growth was the result of Coolidge-style policy. President Ronald Reagan was pulling a Coolidge with a tax reform that brought the top rate down to twenty-eight percent, just three points above that twenty-five percent low-water mark of Coolidge. Even President Bill Clinton did something Coolidge would have liked when he cut the capital gains tax rate in the later 1990s on the bet that the rate cut would bring in extra revenue. It did. Though politicians today rarely recognize it, much of what they do follows the course set by the windsurfer.

Amity Shlaes is a syndicated economic columnist for *Bloomberg*, a senior fellow at the Council on Foreign Relations and author of *The Forgotten Man*, a bestselling history of the Great Depression. She was formerly a columnist for the *Financial Times* and a member of the editorial board of *The Wall Street Journal*. She has been published in the *National Review*, the *New Republic*, *Foreign Affairs* and the *American Spectator*, among other publications. She has twice been a finalist for the Loeb Prize in commentary, and in 2002 she was co-winner of the Frederic Bastiat Prize, an international award for writing on political economy.

Posing with radio and loudspeaker equipment attached to a vehicle used during his Presidential campaign, August 14, 1924.

THE MEDIA
MAESTRO

By Daniel J. Leab

"A visiting magazine writer found Coolidge handled (media) correspondents with a remarkable 'smoothness,' being 'simple, easy and direct.'"

History and historians generally have not been kind to Calvin Coolidge. The image presented of the thirtieth President of the United States is not attractive. One of his first biographers, the noted journalist/editor William Allen White, whose 1938 effort was not unfriendly, characterized Coolidge as a "Puritan in Babylon," a simplistic and unattractive characterization. Since then, Coolidge has not fared much better in print. A generation later, Irving Stone, author of a series of best-selling biographical novels about famous individuals, contributed an article on Coolidge (subtitled "A Study in Inertia") to an anthology about the 1920s and 1930s that a critic described as giving the former President "a vigorous going over, hitting him with a rubber hose.... " Subsequent efforts by such disparate but competent and well-received biographers as Claude Fuess (1940), Donald McCoy (1967), Robert Ferrell (1998), Robert Sobel (1998), and David Greenberg (2006) have been a bit more evenhanded, but even when more positive have not challenged seriously the Coolidge stereotype.

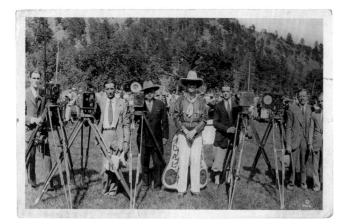

Posing for photographs, dressed as a cowboy July 12, 1927.

The arguments of these writers and others like the journalist and social critic H.L. Mencken are especially geared to Coolidge's public utterances and known activities or lack of activity while in office. Mencken, looking back from the Depression of the 1930s on the *laissez faire* economic policies of the Coolidge Presidency during the 1920s, declared, "Nero fiddled, but Coolidge only snored." Such quips helped to establish the image which, over the decades, has set the tone of critical commentary. Coolidge has been repeatedly characterized as a cold, reticent man who was very sparing with words or actions. The classic story about him is the one that, perhaps apocryphally, deals with a young woman who informs him she has wagered much of her salary on getting him to say to her more than two words; his laconic and crushing response was, "You lose."

To use a phrase utilized by more than one commentator Coolidge was a "minimalist president," one who — as a contemporary warned foreign diplomats — "could be silent in five languages." But even though quite clearly not an outgoing man he certainly was not "Silent Cal" (a scholar estimates that he "wrote or spoke more than seventy-five thousands words" annually during his tenure as President of the United States). He quite deliberately chose to project a certain kind of image, a very limited public persona, while President and earlier in his very successful political career, which began in 1898 when he ran for city council in Northampton, Massachusetts (he won, losing only one election in thirty years). Indeed one biographer calls him a "media virtuoso" who "carefully cultivated" an image from the "moment he entered politics." The President and his advisors downplayed his sentimentality (so obvious in Coolidge's emotional response while in office to the death of his teenaged son,

Calvin, Jr.), his adoration of his wife Grace (a fascinated Washington gossip monger remarked with awe on the fact that the Coolidges slept not only in the same room but in the same bed), his early interests in the classics in their original language, his writing poetry.

There can be no doubt that Coolidge was a particular kind of economic, social and political conservative, one whose policies were not too far removed from those espoused decades later by Ronald Reagan during the 1980s in his Presidency. Reagan much admired Coolidge, an admiration underscored by an act of White House redecorating. Under Reagan's immediate predecessor, the Cabinet Room in the White House had three portraits of previous Presidents (Thomas Jefferson, Abraham Lincoln and Harry Truman); Reagan, after becoming President, replaced the portrait of Truman with one of Coolidge. Reagan maintained, "You hear a lot of jokes about … Coolidge, but I think the joke is on the people that make jokes … if you look at his record." Notwithstanding the differences in the problems that Coolidge and Reagan faced, their approach was often similar and one historian has aptly described Coolidge as a "proto-Reagan."

Certainly, Coolidge — in terms of his day-to-day activities — was much like his 1980s successor in cultivating, and very successfully, the media of the day. Coolidge, like Reagan and many an American conservative figure then and now, had problems with the Left-leaning "chattering classes," but he did manage to win over many of the media rank-and-file, as well as their editors, press lord employers, and other important influential movers and shakers. Coolidge spent many of his weekends in Washington, D.C., after he inherited the Presidency upon Harding's death in 1923, entertaining on the Presidential yacht (a destroyer-sized vessel) and at the White House. The historian Allan Nevins later estimated that Coolidge while President had "more guests" than any previous chief executive.

Typically, when New York politico William J. Donovan, during World War II the founder of the OSS (a forerunner of the CIA), was appointed as Assistant Attorney General in 1924, he and his wife were invited on a cruise up the Potomac. The guests included the Solicitor General and his wife, the Assistant Secretary of the Navy and his wife, and the head of the locally dominant Riggs Bank and his wife. For all Coolidge's noted laconic conversational reticence, which may have come from shyness or natural taciturness as well as deliberate intent, Mrs. Donovan noted in her diary that she had found "the P⸺ ... easy to talk to ... not so difficult as I suspected."

Coolidge worked well with the journalists assigned to cover the activity of the federal government. Even the ones who disagreed with his policies seem to have liked him; as one biographer put it, Coolidge "was good with the press."

Years later, one of the newspapermen who covered Coolidge asserted that, notwithstanding his often sardonic comments to the assembled journalists, "We kinda liked the old coot." Compared to the multi-national herd active currently, the White House in Coolidge's day attracted only a compact homogenous group of about twenty to twenty-five newspapermen on a regular basis. They would gather around the President's desk, in a relatively free give-and-take atmosphere. The President could not be quoted directly, but generally newspaper readers understood just who was speaking when a story was attributed to "a White House spokesman."

It is estimated that Coolidge held five-hundred twenty press conferences, or about eight a month during his nearly six years in office. A visiting magazine writer found Coolidge handled the correspondents with a remarkable "smoothness," being "simple, easy and direct." Policy called for questions to be submitted in advance in writing, but at least one newsman speculated that "I always had the impression that he had not peeked at the questions before we arrived." On the other hand, if Coolidge did not like the questions that had been submitted, he would simply discard the cards or slips of paper he had been given and ignore them. In any event, there was none of the intense preparation of the Chief Executive which now takes place before the much less frequent Presidential press conferences.

Obviously given the importance of newspapers during the Coolidge years, press stories dealing with him and his policies attracted much attention, and strongly

contributed to the creation of that specific public persona — one that was not quite the same as the private man. But just as Reagan did during his Presidential career, all aspects of the media of the day were cultivated. In terms of news photos Coolidge was, as one writer later noted, "probably among the most frequently snapped men of his era." Given the laid-back public persona he had established for himself, the result was often ridiculous and the images were what one historian has described as "bizarre iconographies." But they attest to his intelligent and continued use of yet another branch of the mass media.

Photos such as Coolidge rather forlornly peering out from a full-scale Indian head dress of two-hundred eagle feathers (presented to him by Rosebud Robe, who shortly thereafter would appear in a vaudeville act "as the most beautiful Indian maiden in the world"), fishing in a three-piece suit and wearing waders, or stoically holding a ten-gallon hat while ridiculously dressed in a full cowboy rig, including a set of fancy chaps with "CAL" imprinted upon them (a gift from a group of South Dakota Boy Scouts), all attest to his willingness to do what was necessary to get into the news and the public's eye. Sometimes such efforts backfired: in another widely distributed news photo, which resulted in much comment, a well-groomed President wore a farmer's overalls, but unfortunately his gleamingly polished black city shoes were not cropped out.

Just as Ronald Reagan later mobilized the various branches of the media of the day, so, too, did Coolidge. And, like Reagan, he played them very well. In Coolidge's 1924 campaign for the Presidency, he utilized the services of the fledgling radio industry with its rapidly growing audience. Coolidge's staff arranged for that year's "State of the Union" address to Congress to be broadcast; the Republican

Greeting four Osage Indians at the White House, circa 1925.

Addressing the U.S. House of Representatives, undated.

Party (and later the Democrats) allowed their Presidential conventions also to be broadcast; some weeks after the GOP's June convention renominated Coolidge, he — as was then the case — formally accepted the nomination and his acceptance speech was broadcast; Coolidge ended his 1924 campaign with an election eve broadcast appealing for votes. Altogether Coolidge, who as he put it had "a naturally good radio voice," and recognized that quality, before he left office in March 1929, had given sixteen radio addresses over a five-year period.

Coolidge, a movie fan, previewed new Hollywood feature films for his guests on the Presidential yacht and at the White House, and also made use of this new technology to reach the public. Newsreel cameramen were given the opportunity to film in various unusual situations as well as in the course of more routine activities. Coolidge found it important that there be room for "picture men" (as he dubbed them) during his trips, and was willing to re-enact a situation when necessary, as with presentation of a Congressional medal to Charles Lindbergh after his daring solo flight across the Atlantic in 1927. Coolidge also made use of campaign films and, in their production, was responsive to the ongoing technological innovations: he is the first President recorded speaking on film, doing so in 1926, a year before *The Jazz Singer* premiered, a film whose production is often noted as marking the beginning of sound in the movies.

When Coolidge ran for re-election in 1924, the obvious disarray of a fractured Democratic Party meant his chances were very good. But he and his advisors did not leave matters to chance. Edward Bernays, one of the first practitioners of what became known as "public relations" (and characterized in the *New York Times* as "a master huckster"), was hired to "humanize" Coolidge. As historian Robert Ferrell points out, "it is not certain just what Bernays did" for Coolidge and the ad-man's accounts may be a bit fanciful, but, according to him, the President did understand "the implications of … image making." One Bernays venture was a White House breakfast for a stellar cast of show business personalities. This pseudo-event ended with Al Jolson — a super star of the era — leading a group sing on the White House lawn of the re-election campaign's theme song whose refrain was:

> Keep Coolidge!! Keep Coolidge!!
> And have no fears
> For four more years.
> Keep Coolidge!! Keep Coolidge!!
> For he will right our wrongs!
> He's never asleep
> Still waters run deep.
> So keep Coolidge!! Keep Coolidge!!
> He's right where he belongs!

Coolidge did not choose to run again in 1928 and left the White House in March 1929. And he seems to have had some difficulty in understanding what happened to the nation in the next years, as, following the stock market crash of October 1929, America's economy and society fell victim to increasingly severe hard times. Coolidge, as President, had as one commentator put it "stayed out of the economy and of people's lives." Most of the country had flourished during his Presidency; there had been innumerable references to "Coolidge Prosperity." That era ended as the United States suffered the Great Depression. Whether Coolidge during his Presidency might have acted in ways that would have forestalled the Crash and the Depression was the subject of some dispute among his contemporaries and continues to be debated by some historians of the era. His inactivity had not gone without criticism, but in office he believed the best government was that which governed least, and that is how he functioned.

Sadly, before he died in January 1933, he recognized that his beliefs belonged to the past, and he confided to a friend, "I feel I no longer fit in with these times ... we are in a new era to which I do not belong, and it would not be possible for me to adjust to it." Yet, notwithstanding such views he remained a popular figure, unlike his successor Herbert Hoover, who was despised by many Americans. Coolidge to the surprise of many of the media pundits retained a remarkable level of popularity with the public until his death.

The noted columnist Walter Lippmann — immediately after Coolidge's death, at a time that the country was grinding to halt as it reached the nadir of the Great Depression — noted this "political miracle." With perplexed surprise, Lippmann pointed out that Coolidge's "hold upon the American people ... has endured, though the successes with which he was identified have proved to be illusions and have collapsed."

The almost total collapse of "Coolidge prosperity" did not diminish the affection of the American people for the former President. A Pittsburgh newspaper commenting on his death, without exaggeration, asserted, "Probably no other President ... was as personally popular with all classes of his fellow citizens." Today in 2007, he is neither a figure of fun nor of contempt, if he is remembered at all. For the average person who does recognize the name, he is a former President, but one who does not seem particularly relevant to our times, whatever Ronald Reagan may have thought (perhaps because he, too, is now part of another generation). Still, Coolidge is more than just a waystation between such powerful Presidents as Woodrow Wilson and Franklin D. Roosevelt. It is necessary to understand a time when slogans such as "Keep Cool With Coolidge" and "Coolidge or Chaos" had serious electoral impact.

Many scholars, some of whom view Coolidge negatively and some who do not, think that, whatever Coolidge's beliefs, he was more than the public persona used to sell him to the voters. For intellectuals then and now he has been a figure of fun, but, for many Americans in the heyday of Calvin Coolidge and his Presidency, he was beloved and admired. Perhaps the last word should go to one of his strongest critics. H.L. Mencken had few good words to say about Coolidge during the President's lifetime. Yet after his death Mencken concluded that while "there were no thrills while he reigned ... neither were there any headaches ... he was not a nuisance ... His failings are forgotten. The country remembers only the grateful fact he let it alone. Well, there are worse epitaphs."

Daniel J. Leab, Ph.D., is a Professor of History at Seton Hall University. His essays on popular culture have appeared in various anthologies and include "Coolidge, Hays, and 1920s Movies." For two decades he was editor of the journal *Labor History* and, from 1959 to 1975, he contributed to the *Columbia Journalism Review* in various editorial capacities. His writings have appeared in a variety of publications, including *Monthly Labor Review*, *Historical Journal of Film, Radio, and TV* and *Journalism Quarterly*.

Newspaper industry representatives cheer after the first Coolidge press conference at the White House, August 14, 1923.

HIS VALUES WON
GREATNESS

BY J.R. GREENE

"The values of Calvin Coolidge should be rediscovered by all those who would seek to return the United States to the ideals of its founding and greatness"

W hy is Calvin Coolidge still relevant? Three-quarters of a century after his death, the qualities of the man and his time as President may seem quaint to many Americans. Some view the United States of America as a nation in decline. If that assertion is true, at least some of the blame can be laid at the foot of a culture and society which tend to disregard the ideals and values of individual initiative and honesty, which Coolidge prized so highly.

These values were what created the United States, and allowed it to grow and thrive for its first two centuries of existence. Their steady erosion in the last quarter of the twentieth and early years of the twenty-first Centuries has contributed to the cultural, economic and political travails that have beset the nation since.

Author's note: To provide a framework for the points of this essay, quotes, printed in italics, are used from a eulogy of Coolidge delivered at a meeting of the National Republican Party of Cook County, Illinois, shortly after his death on January 5, 1933.

Portrait with Herbert Hoover, Frank B. Kellogg and representatives of the governments that ratified the Kellogg-Briand Pact — the Treaty for Renunciation of War — in the White House East Room, circa 1925.

The values of Calvin Coolidge should be rediscovered by all those who would seek to return the United States to the ideals of its founding and greatness. Statements by Coolidge, ones about him by contemporaries, and a few facts relating to his political career are used to demonstrate these values.

We shall remember him as ... true to the ideals of the fathers, faithful guardian of those principles of government which constitute our national inheritance.

While he was Governor of Massachusetts, Coolidge stated, "The aim of our government is to protect the weak — to aid them to become strong." As a state senator, he pointed out, "Government cannot relieve from toil."

Coolidge's address on Memorial Day, 1925, included the following words: "The individual, instead of working out his own salvation and securing his own freedom by establishing his own economic and moral independence by his own industry and his own self-mastery, tends to throw himself on some vague influence which he denominates society and to hold that in some way responsible for the sufficiency of his support and the morality of his actions. The local political units likewise look to the states, the states look to the nation, and nations are beginning to look to some vague organization, some nebulous concourse of humanity, to pay their bills and tell them what to do. It is not the method which has made this country what it is. We cannot maintain the Western standard of civilization upon that theory. If it is supported at all, it will have to be supported on the principle of individual responsibility."

In his first annual message to Congress as President, Coolidge observed, "Our Constitution has raised certain barriers against too hasty change. I believe such provision is wise.... The pressing need of the present day is not to change our constitutional rights, but to observe our constitutional rights."

Coolidge ... was called to bring the nation back to [a] creed [of] a national government with will and power to maintain law and order, with liberty and justice, and with life and property safe everywhere; to hold for men and women who toil, the markets their industry creates; to provide credit and currency sound and honest as the good faith and character of the nation.

One of Coolidge's most famous quotes was his reply to a telegram sent by labor leader Samuel Gompers. Gompers sought to restore to their jobs the Boston policemen who had gone out on strike while Coolidge was Governor of Massachusetts in 1919. Coolidge replied, "There is no right to strike against the public safety by anybody, anywhere, any time."

In 1924, John Edgerton, an industrialist, referred to Coolidge as "a man whose essential qualities of mind and soul, and whose unswerving attachment to the fundamentals of free government are going to be demanded by an awakening people in the next President of the United States."

Coolidge's term in office saw the federal government cut income taxes substantially, produce budget surpluses each year, and reduce the national debt by one-third. This was the last time that happened in American history! By the end of Coolidge's term as President, over two-thirds of American citizens didn't have to pay any federal income taxes.

During Coolidge's Presidency, circulating coinage was still in the form of gold and silver (or in currency convertible to them) — sound money. Those metals were removed from our circulating coinage in 1933 and 1970, respectively.

We shall remember him as the patriot, jealous of the honor of his country, devoting his life to her service, loyal to her interests, seeking her welfare, promoting her peace and prosperity, while extending the hand of friendship to all nations of the world.

With Brigadier General John H. Sherburne following the 1919 Boston Police Strike (undated).

In a 1924 address to members of the press, Coolidge stated his basic principles on foreign affairs: "On what nations are at home depends what they will be abroad. If the spirit of freedom rules in their domestic affairs, it will rule in their foreign affairs. The world knows that we do not seek to rule by force of arms, our strength is in our moral power. We increase the desire for peace everywhere by being peaceful. We maintain a military force for our defense, but our offensive lies in the justice of our cause. We are against war because it is destructive. We are for peace because it is constructive. We seek concord with all nations through mutual understanding."

In another 1924 address, Coolidge stated, "We have a well-defined foreign policy … it has as its foundations peace with independence."

The Kellogg-Briand Peace Pact was signed near the end of Coolidge's term. While it is looked upon today as having been a naïve step at best, it confirmed Coolidge's view of using negotiation and arbitration to settle disputes between nations.

We shall remember him for his spotless character, the man with clean hands and pure heart who through his plighted word was to his heart, changed it not; whose integrity was firm and rugged as the granite in the hills of his native state.

In his address of acceptance of nomination as the Republican Party's standard bearer in 1924, Coolidge stated: "Underneath and upholding political parties was, and is, the enduring principle that a true citizen of a real republic cannot exist as a segregated, unattached fragment of selfishness, but must live as a constituent part of the whole of society, in which he can secure his own welfare only as he secures the welfare of his fellow men."

In the wake of the Teapot Dome scandals, Congress sought to investigate the activities of Attorney General Harry Daugherty. When the latter refused to hand over certain papers sought by Congress, Coolidge asked for, and received, his resignation. Coolidge also appointed a Republican and a Democrat as special counsels to investigate those scandals.

[He was] the leader who discerned the spiritual values … who above the rush and roar of commerce saw a vision of the righteousness which exalts a nation.

Coolidge, in one of his addresses, pointed out, "We make no concealment of the fact that we want wealth, but there are many other things we want very much more. We want peace and honor, and that charity which is so strong an element of all civilization. The chief ideal of the American people is idealism. I cannot repeat too often that America is a nation of idealists."

Dwight Morrow, Coolidge's classmate at Amherst College, and appointee as Ambassador to Mexico, called Coolidge a "very unusual man and a strange combination of a transcendental philosopher, and a practical politician."

While addressing the Roman Catholic Holy Name Society in 1924 (during the height of national influence of the Ku Klux Klan), Coolidge stated, "We Americans are idealists. We are willing to follow the truth solely because it is the truth. We put our main emphasis on the things which are spiritual. While we possess an unsurpassed skill in marshalling and using the material resources of the world, still the nation has not sought for wealth and power as an end but as a means to a higher life."

Honesty, thrift and spiritual values were all ideals that meant so much to Calvin Coolidge, and they need to be revived in American culture for the nation to regain its greatness.

J.R. Greene is the author of 15 books and numerous articles on historical subjects. His three books on Calvin Coolidge are: *Calvin Coolidge: A Biography in Picture Postcards* (1987), *Calvin Coolidge's Plymouth Vermont* (1997) and *A Bibliography of Pamphlets Relating to Calvin Coolidge, 1910–1988* (1989). He is a lifelong resident of Athol, Massachusetts.

As guests of honor at the Tercentenary Celebration at Watertown, Massachusetts (undated).

America Needs a New Coolidge

By John F. Kerry

"America needs a Calvin Coolidge today to restore our faith in the office of the Presidency and in politics more generally."

When President Warren G. Harding died of a heart attack in the summer of 1923, the Presidency that Calvin Coolidge inherited was in tatters after a scandal-plagued administration. As four-term New York Governor and 1928 Democratic Presidential candidate Alfred E. Smith wrote, Coolidge's "great task was to restore the dignity and prestige of the Presidency when it had reached the lowest ebb in our history ... in a time of extravagance and waste."

In his inimitably taciturn manner, "Silent Cal" did just that.

Upon taking office, he opened government to the people. He pledged to meet with reporters twice a week and root out corruption in the administration he was inheriting. His actions matched his words.

Coolidge was nothing like the polished, rhetoric-laden politicians of today. He was reserved, introspective and a man of few words. He earned his moniker, "Silent Cal," when a woman approached him at a dinner party and said she had made a wager against a fellow who said it was impossible to get more than two words out of him. Coolidge's response? "You lose."

Being informed of his nomination for Lieutenant Governor of Massachusetts, circa 1915.

In reality, he was only personally a man of few words. When it came to the responsibilities of discharging his office, he gave numerous press conferences and wrote his own speeches. There wasn't much spin coming out of the White House then, since Coolidge himself was somewhat of a one man communications department.

While Americans in the twenty-first century might question the ability of a Coolidge-like Chief Executive to handle the crises of the day, in 1923 he was exactly what the nation needed to restore trust in government. His reputation for integrity and his principled governance spoke for itself.

The naked corruption of the Harding Administration has few equals in our history. Several of Harding's appointees were convicted for accepting bribes. The most infamous case was the Teapot Dome scandal, in which Secretary of the Interior Albert B. Fall took bribes and illegal zero-interest loans in exchange for the lease of public oil fields.

When President Harding died on August 2, 1923, Secretary of State Evans Hughes urged Vice President Coolidge to take his oath of office immediately. Coolidge was visiting his family in Vermont at the time. His father, as a Notary Public, swore him into office.

"I was awakened by my father coming up the stairs calling my name. I noticed that his voice trembled," Coolidge wrote. "He placed in my hand an official report and told me that President Harding had just passed away."

President Coolidge understood the task before him. As a young man, when his father took him to hear President Benjamin Harrison speak, he "wondered how it felt to bear so much responsibility and little thought I should ever know." But he knew well what the country then needed. He said, "Observance of the law ensures the rights of man. The right thing to do never requires any subterfuge. It is always simple and direct."

Expectations were high. "The welfare of the country is critically dependent upon the success of President Coolidge," wrote Chief Justice Taft to Treasury Secretary Andrew Mellon. But Coolidge did not shrink from the task. "When a duty comes to us," he said, "with it a power comes to enable us to perform it."

Though he was of the same party, Coolidge purged the Executive branch of Harding's corrupt administration and did not let those who had committed crimes escape punishment. "The sole guarantee of liberty is obedience to law under the forms of ordered government," he said.

Calvin Coolidge also showed a praiseworthy commitment to peacemaking in American foreign relations by signing the Kellogg-Briand Pact of 1928, which committed major powers in Europe and Asia to "renounce war, as an instrument of national policy in their relations with one another." Though history shows that the Kellogg-Briand pact did not have its exact desired effect, it became a founding principle of international law.

In looking at Coolidge's long list of Presidential accomplishments, it's important to note that his legacy rose out of years of building leadership and trust in state and local politics.

He was born in Vermont, but we are proud to consider him an adopted son of Massachusetts. He left his family home to attend Amherst College and, after graduating, he practiced law in Massachusetts. He then worked his way up from a seat on the City Council of Northampton to the state legislature. After serving as a popular Senate President, he was elected Lieutenant Governor of the Commonwealth — a job I myself held — and then Governor.

Coolidge explained his philosophy of government to the public with his well-received speech, *Have Faith in Massachusetts*: "Do the day's work. If it be to protect the rights of the

Homecoming Parade in Northampton, Massachusetts following his nomination for Vice President of the United States, June 1920.

weak, whoever objects, do it. If it be to help a powerful corporation to better serve the people, whatever be the opposition, do that. Expect to be called a stand-patter, but don't be a stand-patter. Expect to be called a demagogue, but don't be a demagogue.... Don't expect to build up the weak by tearing down the strong. Recognize the mortal worth and the dignity of man."

Coolidge's belief in peace, accountability and integrity continues to be as important today as during his term. And whether Republican or Democrat, America needs a Calvin Coolidge today to restore our faith in the office of the Presidency and in politics more generally.

"The only way I know to drive out evil from the country is by the constructive method of filling it with good. The country is better off tranquilly considering its blessing and merits, and earnestly striving to secure more of them, than it would be in nursing hostile bitterness about it deficiencies and faults," Coolidge said.

John F. Kerry is a four-term United States Senator from Massachusetts. He served as Chairman of the Senate Committee on Small Business and Entrepreneurship. Senator Kerry was also the 2004 Presidential nominee for the Democratic Party. A Vietnam combat veteran and former district attorney, he served as Lieutenant Governor of the Commonwealth of Massachusetts — a position once held by Calvin Coolidge.

October 22, 1924

With Mrs. Coolidge and American labor and community activist Mother Jones (center) circa 1924

A Champion of Women's Rights

By Cynthia D. Bittinger

"He encouraged women and their aspirations in every field of our modern era."

On May 8, 1931, former President Calvin Coolidge wrote about Mother's Day in his syndicated column: "It is hard to imagine a greater ambition than to be what our mothers would wish us to be.... None of us can give as much as our mothers gave to us." In terms of a partner, he wrote to Bruce Barton in 1926, "A man who has the companionship of a lovely and gracious woman enjoys the supreme blessing that life can give." He also said, "What men owe to the love and help of good women can never be told." Obviously Calvin Coolidge appreciated the women in his family.

He also appreciated women in the wider world. Growing up in a rural community where gender was not as limiting as in the country's urban, stratified society, he could envision women making contributions in different occupations. Calvin Coolidge set a good example and that is one reason why he matters to this modern world. He saw the progress women were making in forming clubs and influencing legislation, and, of course, he and Warren Harding were the first Presidential team to be voted into office when women were given the right to vote in 1920. He also respected the Prohibition

With son Calvin Jr. and father John at the family farm.

movement, largely led by women, since he could see in his own town how strongly women felt about the evils of drink. Women were making progress and he respected that. When he could, he assisted in their drive for equality.

Coolidge supported women's suffrage from the first, in 1907. That is to his credit. His opponents were often against giving the vote to women and they were targeted by activist groups. Coolidge became president of the Massachusetts Senate when the former Senate president, Levi H. Greenwood, was defeated for his anti-women stance. From the Senate, Coolidge supported the Mothers' Relief Bill. As governor, he signed the forty-eight-hour bill to safeguard women and children.

In the 1920s, women were appointed to special federal commissions and committees. More women became postmasters (Calvin's town of Plymouth hired his stepmother Carrie Brown as postmaster). Female professional social scientists lobbied to achieve the 1921 Shepard-Towner legislation, the act which established the first health grants in aid program under the Children's Bureau with a goal of a network of states administering programs to improve the health of mothers and infants.

After fighting for civil rights for African-Americans, the rights of women were a priority for the Republican Party. "Women have been active in the Republican party since its founding days," according to historian Melanie Gustafson. The first women in Congress were Republicans, and, in 1918, the U.S. House passed the Susan B. Anthony amendment with two-hundred Republican votes, one-hundred and two Democratic. In 1919, when the U.S. Senate voted for the amendment, the majority of votes were from Republicans. At the GOP conventions, women were represented with twenty-seven delegates in 1920 and one-hundred twenty in 1924.

President Calvin Coolidge knew the women from Vermont at the 1924 convention. The Vermont delegation included his cousin, Blanche Brown Bryant, who sat in the front row. The Vermont women marched in long lines to shout for

Coolidge and stood on chairs to wave banners. As Bryant wrote, "It was a gay and exciting time, as well as an opening into the world of political science — a rewarding and memorable experience."

The nominating speech for Calvin Coolidge in 1924, given by Dr. Marion L. Burton of Michigan, was a strong endorsement of him as a man who understood the importance of women in the role of the nation. Burton's thesis was that women belonged in politics and that "we do not want solely a man's or a woman's world — we want a human world and we are rapidly achieving it."

During the Twenties, women's clubs were formed to provide institutional support; the Women's National Republican Club was established in 1921. Helen Varick Boswell was with the West End Women's Republican Club and president of the Women's Forum in New York. In 1929, Calvin Coolidge appointed her to represent the United States at the International Exposition in Spain. Coolidge's convention in 1924 was a high point for female participation at the time with twenty-five women on four convention committees. This was not repeated again until 1944. Women were speakers at both conventions, giving seconding speeches for Presidential candidates. The 1920 platform endorsed the establishment of a Women's Bureau in the Department of Labor, the principle of equal pay for equal work for federal workers, the special needs of women workers for vocational training, and legislation regulating working hours for women in certain industrial jobs.

In 1924, Calvin Coolidge recognized the role of women in the nation and wanted them to vote! In his acceptance speech, he said, "I know the influence of womanhood will guard the home, which is the citadel of the nation. I know it will be a protector of childhood, I know it will be on the side of humanity. I welcome it as a great instrument of mercy and a mighty agency of peace. I want every woman to vote."

With the "First Lady of Law" Assistant U.S. Attorney General Mabel Walker Willebrandt and Congressman Israel Moore "I.M." Foster, June 7, 1924.

African-American women flocked to the party with Mary Church Terrell leading the charge. After all, this was the party of Lincoln, McKinley and Theodore Roosevelt. The women's peace movement was a major force behind the 1929 Kellogg-Briand Pact, Coolidge's attempt to end war through international law.

Consuelo Bailey of Vermont credited Mabel Walker Willebrandt, Assistant Attorney General of the United States under Coolidge, as inspiring her when she spoke at Boston University's law school where Bailey was attending. Bailey was a devoted fan of Calvin Coolidge noting his "taciturnity, humility and thriftiness." She wrote, in her autobiography, that "these qualities were not a part of him; they were Calvin Coolidge. They could not be separated from him any more than the echo of the thunder as it has rolled back and forth for centuries through the mountains which glorify the horizon at Plymouth Notch." Bailey, in 1926, became the seventh woman to practice law in Vermont, the first woman to become the state's Attorney of Chittenden County, and went on to become the first elected female lieutenant governor in the country in 1954! She told the story that Calvin Coolidge was once told that no women had been on the U.S. Customs Court of New York and that he replied, "No one will ever say that again." He appointed Genevieve Rose Cline to the seat. Bailey was a founder along with many other national leaders of the Calvin Coolidge Memorial Foundation in 1960.

Mabel Walker Willebrandt, appointed by President Harding, was the first woman Assistant Attorney General in the nation with the unpopular job of enforcing prohibition. She also was responsible for federal income tax litigation and the federal prison system. She argued cases before the Supreme Court and was a key advocate for prison reform. She set the basic interpretations of the new 16th and 18th amendments. Yet her role in the Coolidge administration is seldom acknowledged in contemporary essays.

The twentieth century became the century for women to find their rightful place in the life of the American republic. Modern America came of age between 1890 and 1920. A new demographic of "college-educated, frequently unmarried, and self-supporting" women emerged. For instance, the women's club movement in Chicago pushed for reforms such as the Legal Aid Society, the Public Art Association, and the Protective Agency for Women and Children.

Fashions were changing and Victorian ideas were challenged. Calvin was pleased that his wife wore fashionable clothes and took long walks for her health. Her love of baseball made it clear to him that sports were becoming an important part of society and that women were often participants.

Calvin and Grace Coolidge joined Florence and Warren Harding and Lou and Herbert Hoover to feature art and to showcase music at the White House. The First Ladies organized concerts in the garden, and arts became their sphere in the 1920s. Grace Coolidge made a point of inviting women at the top of their fields and was sure they would serve as role models for future generations.

Calvin Coolidge appreciated women's contributions to the family and society as well as politics. His example is a fine one for today's world. He grew up observing women participating in non-traditional roles in his town of Plymouth and noted that strong women often ruled the day. He shared responsibilities in his companionate marriage, learned to trust his wife's instincts to manage the social side of the White House, and supported her drive to raise funds to help educate deaf children. He also was able to appoint women to new positions in the government and seemed proud to be able to do this. His friendship with important women of his times, Mother Jones, Helen Keller and Carrie Chapman Catt, was real. As much as Coolidge wanted to be "one of us," he really did speak to the better side of mankind. He encouraged women and their aspirations in every field of our modern era.

Cynthia D. Bittinger is the former Executive Director of The Calvin Coolidge Memorial Foundation in Plymouth, Vermont. Her biography on First Lady Grace Coolidge is entitled *Grace Coolidge, Sudden Star*. She is on the editorial board of *White House Studies* and wrote the biographical profile for Grace Coolidge in *American First Ladies*. Her commentaries on Calvin and Grace Coolidge won a Vermont Associated Press award and a commendation award from the American Association for State and Local Historical Societies in 2004.

With Mrs. Coolidge, their two sons, John and Calvin Jr., Vice President and Mrs. Dawes, Coolidge family friend Frank W. Stearn, and Supreme Court Justice Pierce Butler, June 30, 1924.

BREVITY GAVE HIM POWER

By Melanie Gustafson

"For him the line between public and private was solid. It may be one of his most enduring political legacies."

One can't help but like Calvin Coolidge after reading his 1929 autobiography. In seven short chapters Coolidge sketches out the "persistent and painstaking work" that led him from a boyhood in rural Vermont to the pinnacle of political power as President of the United States. He provides snapshots of the individuals who influenced and encouraged him, and of those who supported his political aspirations. His highest praise goes to his parents and grandparents, and to the rural Vermont that shaped his ideals. He writes of his father that the "work he did endured" and of his Vermont that "little about it was artificial." Coolidge detested all things artificial.

His autobiography is crafted in a traditional way, moving chronologically, hitting the highpoints of public life, reaffirming his love of his family. He writes not to settle old scores; opponents are dismissed not by name but with explanations of the incorrectness of their ideas. He does not seem concerned with promoting his post-Presidential celebrity or securing his legacy. He wants his book to be useful. He tells us that he hopes his autobiography will "prove to be an encouragement to others in their struggles

Taking an oath prior to casting his ballot in the 1924 Presidential election, circa 1924.

to improve their place in the world." His message about how this effort should happen and what this improvement means is simple. Advancement and success come to those who lead a life of measured restraint and persistent hard work. Throughout the book he emphasizes that one should resist those aspects of modern life that promote frivolity instead of honesty, cynicism over optimism, and the quest for material accumulation more than the responsibility to live judiciously.

"Unless we live rationally," he wrote, "we perish, physically, mentally, spiritually." However one assesses Coolidge's policies or agenda, his message about individual and civic responsibility is as important today as it was in 1929.

Not surprisingly, Coolidge makes every word count in his autobiography. He captures the essence of a twelve-year-old boy's grief at the death of his mother with one strong sentence: "Life was never to seem the same again." His reflections on the deaths of his sixteen-year-old son Calvin, Jr. and beloved father John are equally powerful: "I do not know why such a price was exacted for occupying the White House. It costs a great deal to be President." Tens of thousands of telegrams of condolence were sent to the White House when Calvin, Jr. died in July 1924. Newspapers ran articles that fed the public's intense interest in the children of Presidents. Stories about the death of Calvin, Jr. morphed into ones about eleven-year-old Willie Lincoln, who died in 1862, and into other tales whose shared motif was a parent's grief. Calvin Coolidge, ever economical with words, let his wife Grace respond to the public's sympathies. The President kept his sorrow within himself and in his family circle.

This makes his autobiographical comments about these times of sadness even more compelling.

H.L. Mencken once stated that Coolidge's "self-revelations have been so few and so wary that it is even difficult to guess. No august man of his station has talked about himself less." Coolidge's refusal, or inability, to reveal his private thoughts have frustrated observers. Exasperation grows when one realizes how much material he provided us. Coolidge enthusiastically embraced the medium of radio, willingly spoke with reporters, and appeared effortlessly in front of the camera. To understand Coolidge better, we need to remind ourselves that he held one of the most visible public positions at the cultural moment when the line between public and private was increasingly blurred, when news and entertainment technologies allowed for and encouraged the commodification and consumption of the private lives of public individuals. While Coolidge embraced the new political culture of the day by hiring the country's best public relations teams to run his campaign and take care of aspects of his Presidency, he also held firm in his belief that some things were private. This was a principled position. For him the line between public and private was solid. It may be one of his most enduring political legacies.

Still, Coolidge was an astute politician. He understood that a public figure is the very embodiment of his ideas. So, even as he gave speech after speech, he encouraged the image of the President of few words and contributed to the enduring iconic persona of "Silent Cal."

In the noisy world of the 1920s, where radio and newsreels joined newspapers and magazines to communicate information and entertain the masses, Coolidge's silence was notable. It provided a space within the cacophony whereby his specific verbal and visual messages could resonate. On the surface, those messages were about encouraging economic growth, but, in more subtle ways, they sought to instill in Americans the cultural values that Coolidge embraced: thrift, hard work, and perseverance.

Everyone knows the story of the hostess who challenged Coolidge that she could make him say more than two words. She lost. My favorite story is from the moment that women won the right to vote. A Republican

At the White House with members of the New York Women's Republican Club.

woman delegate asked the Vice Presidential nominee to give her a message she could take to voters about the need for cooperation between the sexes. According to the *New York Times*, Coolidge responded by contemplating the floor. "Thinking she had not been heard, the lady repeated her battle cry for cooperation. Still Coolidge gazed abstractedly. As the lady was on the point of turning away she is said to have distinguished three syllables, murmured in a metallic undertone: 'Can-be-done.' " There was a lot of noise, a lot of press, about how men and women were going to — or maybe not — work together in politics after 1920. Coolidge cut through the noise with his usual optimism.

Coolidge's autobiography reads like a Horatio Alger novel. Between 1867 and the late 1890s, Alger published hundreds of stories about poor boys who triumphed over adversity. These rags-to-riches stories were incredibly popular with a generation of young men who sought to advance themselves by moving from the rural countryside to urban areas. This was Coolidge's generation. The central trope in these stories — that hard work and perseverance lead to success — was one of Coolidge's primary messages to the next generation. Both Alger and Coolidge believed, and wanted us to believe, that some values are timeless, are necessary for community prosperity and harmony, and are essential for a good society.

Luck also plays an important role in the Horatio Alger novels. On the path to success, the boys find themselves in just the right place at just the right time to win the notice of successful older men who offer them help. To these men, the boys are always loyal. Coolidge comes closest to acknowledging the role of luck in a man's life when he wrote in his autobiography, "If one will only exercise the patience to wait, his wants are likely to be filled." "Coolidge luck" was a more prominent theme in media reports of the era. One 1924 *New York Times* article, written when the new women voters were still unique enough to be noteworthy, attributed Coolidge's success to "lady" luck. Its headline declared that a "Suffragette Cleared the Way for Coolidge's Rise to Power" and related the story of Boston's Margaret Foley who, in 1913, worked to defeat Levi Greenwood's reelection because he opposed woman suffrage. Greenwood's defeat allowed

Coolidge to make his successful bid for President of the Massachusetts Senate, a position that, Coolidge tells us, transformed him from a "purely local figure" into a man with "state-wide distinction and authority."

Considering his penchant for brevity, Coolidge recalls this series of events with an extravagant number of words in his autobiography, and he emphasizes his tenacity in gathering the necessary pledges to win the election. The *Times* story also notes this doggedness but places greater emphasis on the element of luck. If women were not dedicated to winning the right to vote and if Miss Foley had not helped to defeat the anti-suffragist Greenwood, Calvin Coolidge would not have been elected President of the Massachusetts Senate and would not have given an inaugural speech that captured the attention of Frank W. Stearns. This man, like a character in a Horatio Alger story, appears out of nowhere and would help Coolidge complete his rags-to-riches story. What was it in that speech that so captivated Stearns? Maybe it was these words: "Be loyal to the commonwealth and to yourselves. And be brief. Above all things, be brief."

Melanie Gustafson is a historian and author of *Women and the Republican Party, 1854-1924*. She is also the co-editor of *We Have Come to Stay: American Women and Political Parties, 1880-1960* and *Major Problems in the History of World War II*. She edits the *American Women's Biography* series for the University of New Mexico Press, and is well known for writing *Becoming a Historian: A Survival Guide*, published by the American Historical Association.

Chief Justice William H. Taft administers the oath of office on the east portico of the U.S. Capitol, March 4, 1925.

A STICKLER FOR THE RULE OF LAW

By Russell Fowler

"The record of Calvin Coolidge's Presidency ... provides wisdom worth retrieving today."

The manner in which Calvin Coolidge became President of the United States on the 3rd of August, 1923, upon the unexpected death of President Warren G. Harding, gave an aura of humility and traditional values in stark contrast with his predecessor's administration and its soon-to-be discovered corruptions. By the light of a kerosene lamp, Coolidge's father, in his capacity as a Notary, administered the Presidential oath of office at the Coolidge family farm at Plymouth Notch, Vermont, at 2:47 a.m. Following the ceremony, Coolidge returned to his bedroom, prayed a while on his knees and went back to sleep as America's thirtieth President. When he awoke later that morning, he visited his mother's grave, then headed for Washington.

The simple, yet dramatic event captivated the country and helped to create a groundswell of support for the new Chief Executive as he forged an administration and deftly confronted the unprecedented scandals of Harding's "Ohio gang." Coolidge's political skill fast became apparent. Between becoming President and the 1924 Republican Convention less than a year later, he purged the discredited

The 1925 inaugural parade, March 4, 1925.

Harding regime (including the firing of the Attorney General), assured prosecution of the wrongdoers, effectively disassociated his party from the scandals, and took control of the party machinery. The GOP joyfully surrendered to the dominance of the "Puritan in Babylon," for he had been all that stood between it and political oblivion. "He is keenly as good a politician as Lincoln," happily proclaimed Chief Justice William Howard Taft.

Coolidge's accessibility and use of the press — through frequent press conferences, colorful photo events, and regular radio speeches among other displays — in an odd way made "Silent Cal" the first media President. Not only had the damage from the Harding scandals been limited, he swiftly managed his policies, pronouncements and public image so as to become the personification of integrity. In his silence, he seemed to hover above petty politics, and, the less he said, the more noticed were the few words he spoke.

Even opposition leaders such as Democratic Presidential nominee John W. Davis and Franklin Roosevelt begrudgingly praised him. As Roosevelt confessed, "To rise superior to Coolidge will be a hard thing." In contrast to Davis, Coolidge did little campaigning, partly due to the inevitability of his election and the death of his youngest son, age 16, from blood poisoning resulting from a blister on his toe formed while playing tennis on the White House lawn. Coolidge wrote, "When he went, the power and the glory of the Presidency went with him." Yet by the summer of 1924, "The Quiet President" could survey the political landscape and behold no threats. The same was not true for Chief Justice Taft.

Senator Robert "Fighting Bob" La Follette won the Progressive Party Presidential nomination and began an energetic albeit hopeless campaign. Although attacking administration labor and farm policies and calling for the nationalization of railroads, La Follette's most radical proposals concerned the federal judiciary. Angered over injunctions against strikers and Supreme Court rulings declaring pro-labor laws unconstitutional, La Follette called for the election of federal judges, the preclusion of lower courts from declaring federal laws unconstitutional, and the empowering of Congress to overturn decisions of the Supreme Court.

The President finally decided that responding to La Follette was expedient, and defending the sanctity of the courts was in keeping with Coolidge's favorite topic of political discourse: the rule of law. He also had growing concerns about a general lack of respect for the law, and more specifically, the rise of organized criminal activity benefiting from Prohibition and a resurgent Ku Klux Klan in the South and Mid-West.

In one of his few campaign speeches, the President unveiled in Baltimore a central theme of his campaign: defense of the law and courts. Coolidge declared that an independent judiciary headed by a Supreme Court is one of "the greatest contributions which America made to the science of government ... with the sole purpose of protecting the freedom of the individual, of guarding his earnings, his home, his life." He further explained why judicial power should not be "transferred in whole or in part to the Congress" because of its acquiescence to "popular demand" and "partisan advantage." In a subsequent address, Coolidge alleged that La Follette's plan "would be a device more nearly calculated to take away the rights of the people and leave them subject to all the influences which might be exerted on the Congress by the power and wealth of vested interests on one day and the passing whim of popular passion on another day." In response, editorial pages and political cartoonists portrayed the President as the guardian of constitutionalism.

As historian Paul Johnson observed, "He thought the essence of the republic was not so much democracy itself as the rule of law and the prime function of government was to uphold and enforce it." As Coolidge himself said, "But in resisting all attacks upon our liberty, you will always remember that the sole guarantee of liberty is obedience to law under the forms of ordered government." Or, as stated in his 1925 inaugural address, "In a republic the first rule for the guidance of the citizen is obedience to law." He believed that this is what distinguishes America from the "forces of darkness."

As Governor of Massachusetts, his strong stand during the Boston police strike of 1919, and his mobilization of the state guard to restore calm, demonstrated his dedication to law and order. During the height of the turmoil, his famous telegram to AFL leader Samuel Gompers stating, "There is no right to strike against the public safety by anybody, anywhere, any time," gave Coolidge national prominence, and he easily won re-election as Governor based on his defense of the rule of law.

As President, Coolidge's commitment to enforce the law led him to vigorously enforce Prohibition as the law of the land despite his misgivings about its wisdom. He also did not hesitate to issue a secret order commanding the Internal Revenue Services to go after Chicago gangster Al Capone. It was this directive, not so much the exploits of the FBI's "Untouchables," that proved to be the ultimate undoing of the mob kingpin. In foreign affairs, Coolidge signed the idealistic Kellogg-Briand Pact outlawing war as an instrument of national policy, sent 5,000 troops to Nicaragua to maintain order, and went against many in the GOP and Congress in supporting American participation in the new World Court. Also, although often overlooked, Coolidge's dedication to the rule of law included his longstanding concern for the civil and economic rights of black Americans. As Coolidge biographer Robert Sobel noted, "Few presidents were as outspoken on the need to protect the civil rights of black Americans as Calvin Coolidge."

There was nothing new about Coolidge's interest in human rights and his intertwining of those rights with the rule of law and democracy. As early as 1914, he urged the Massachusetts Senate to "Recognize the immortal worth and dignity of man. ... Such is the path to equality before the law. Such is the foundation of liberty under the law. Such is the sublime revelation of man's relation to man — Democracy." He was also willing to back up words with action. In 1915, despite praise for the motion picture by President Woodrow Wilson, Coolidge tried to ban in Boston the showing of the racist, pro-Klan film "The Birth of a Nation." As Vice President, he had warned, "We need to learn and exemplify the principle of toleration. We are a nation of many races and of many beliefs."

During the 1924 campaign President Coolidge spoke at Howard University and, in clear criticism of the Ku Klux Klan, denounced "the propaganda of prejudice and hatred" and praised the contributions of African Americans in World War I. As in his first message to Congress in 1923, he included language in his party's platform calling for strong federal anti-lynching laws so that "the full influence of the federal government may be wielded to exterminate the hideous crime." This was the precursor of later federal efforts to secure the civil rights of blacks in the South. The GOP platform also reflected his desire that a federal commission be created to investigate the "social and economic conditions" of black Americans and promote "mutual understanding and confidence."

Coolidge personally urged black Republicans to run for public office, provided extensive patronage to black political leaders in the South, and repeatedly sought federal funding of medical school scholarships for black students. He was "much troubled by insistent discrimination" against black Justice Department employees. Calling their treatment "a terrible thing," he commanded the Attorney General at a cabinet meeting "to find a way to give them an even chance." Coolidge summed up his view: "We all live in the same world. We are bound to a common destiny through a common brotherhood."

Although these stands may have been "politically imprudent" considering the times, the President never wavered in his commitment to civil rights and used the 1924 campaign to advance this cause. He put commitment behind his words, "One with the law is a majority." On election day, voters decided to follow the advice of the campaign slogan and "Keep Cool with Coolidge." The extent of the President's landslide stunned even his most ardent supporters. He would also be the last

John Calvin Coolidge, Sr., President Coolidge's father, reads a telegram announcing funeral plans for his grandson, Calvin Coolidge III, circa 1924.

Congratulating Mississippi River hero Thomas Lee, who saved the lives of 32 passengers of the sinking steamboat M.E. Norman, May 28, 1925.

incumbent Republican occupant of the White House to win a majority of the black vote.

After the 1924 election, Coolidge turned to giving further proof to his declaration in the belief in the rule of law. He successfully pressured Congress to enact the "Judges' Bill" of 1925. Along with other major reforms making the system more efficient and fair, this landmark measure granted the Supreme Court wide discretion regarding the cases accepted for review. Justices freed from routine appeals could concentrate on important constitutional and federal law questions. Moreover, it helped to open the federal courts to those previously excluded. In the future, when progressives failed to achieve their agenda in Congress and state legislatures, such as securing civil rights and liberties, they would increasingly turn to the federal courts because of judicial reforms achieved by Coolidge.

Further reflecting his deep concern for the fair administration of justice, Coolidge gave extraordinary scrutiny to evaluating potential judicial nominees. Reflecting the importance he placed on the subject, he was very secretive, not even discussing potential selections with his closest advisors, but would carefully consider views of bar and community leaders in the jurisdiction of the vacancy. On a number of occasions Coolidge resisted political pressure to appoint senators' favorites to judicial posts. One historian has noted, "Few Presidents have set for themselves higher standards for appointees or acted more independently of solicitors." And it was concluded, "Coolidge seldom played politics, but tried honestly to select the best available candidate. A careful study of his appointments will show that he was seldom influenced by partisan motives, party man though he was."

As early as his famous "Have Faith in Massachusetts" speech of 1914, given on his election as President of the Massachusetts Senate, Coolidge proclaimed the value of courts free of politics saying, "Courts are established, not to determine the popularity of a cause, but to adjudicate and enforce rights. No litigant should be required to submit his case to the hazard and expense of a political campaign. No judge should be required to seek or receive political rewards. The courts of Massachusetts are known and honored wherever men love justice. Let their glory suffer no diminution at our hands. The electorate and the judiciary cannot combine. A hearing means a hearing. When the trial of a cause goes outside the courtroom, Anglo-Saxon constitutional government ends."

Although most of his appointees were Republican and judicial conservatives, legal merit overrode political influence and ideological purity. As Coolidge said, "The public service would be improved if all vacancies were filled by simply appointing the best ability and character that can be found. That is what is done in private business." By comparison, President Franklin Roosevelt used district court judgeships to reward local politicians. Ironically, New Deal agency lawyers confessed that they preferred Coolidge's to FDR's judges, for although politically conservative, they were usually better lawyers and thus "more willing to accept a reasoned argument and enforce the law."

Coolidge's most notable judicial appointment was that of Harlan Fiske Stone to the Supreme Court of the United States, his only Supreme Court appointment. Demonstrating the bi-partisan acclaim for Stone, President Roosevelt subsequently elevated Stone to the Chief Justiceship. Coolidge's successor, Herbert Hoover, later considered offering Coolidge a future vacancy on the Supreme Court. Yet, if offered, it would have been declined. Coolidge was tired and wanted to be home in Northampton, Massachusetts, as first made public in 1927 by his one-sentence press release: "I do not choose to run for President in nineteen twenty-eight." Thus he left office with his popularity intact and with the knowledge he could have had another term if sought. On his last day in the White House, he told a friend, "It is a pretty good idea to get out when they still want you."

It may seem strange that Americans turned so enthusiastically to the reserved, frugal Calvin Coolidge for leadership during "the Roaring Twenties."

But like their President, most Americans sensed the growing disrespect for the restraints of society such as religion and tradition, and witnessed the blatant rejection of the restraints of law by gangsters, corrupt politicians, Klansmen, and Communists. And with all the changes going on in America in the 1920s, as the nation transitioned from a predominately rural to urban society and modern American culture was born, there came the uncertainty and nervousness born from conflict between the lifestyles of the past and an unfamiliar and rambunctious present. President Coolidge served as the calming counterbalance and the comforting link to a simpler past and its values. But there was more to Coolidge's triumph than image and timing.

The real key to understanding Coolidge's remarkable career and his political philosophy is his belief in the rule of law and his ability to express and implement it. His efforts to achieve the benefits of the rule of law — security, stability and liberty — demonstrate that he was an able and active administrator, truly interested in individual freedom, racial tolerance, and open and impartial courts.

As the Great Depression deepened in the 1930s and Republican fortunes fell, the former President's popularity never diminished, as many longed for a return to the days of "the Coolidge prosperity." There was even talk of drafting him for the 1932 Republican nomination, as if retrieving its symbol could revive an era, but as he wrote, "I know my work is done." His wife found him dead of a heart attack at his Northampton home at the age of sixty in January of 1933. He was buried beside his son on a quiet hillside at Plymouth Notch.

Democrat Al Smith concluded that Coolidge's "great task was to restore the dignity and prestige of the Presidency when it had reached the lowest ebb in our history, and to afford, in a time of extravagance and waste, a shining example of the simple and homely virtues which came down to him from his New England ancestors. These are no small achievements, and history will not forget them."

The passage of time and the prejudices of historians has often obscured President Coolidge's legacy. Historians usually demand the backdrop of great events — wars and revolutions — as a prerequisite for affixing greatness, and Calvin Coolidge's administration, a respite of peace and plenty, fell between the dramas of world war and depression. But perhaps there are times when healing is a greater virtue than reform, and restoration and respectability more valuable than revolution. Perhaps giving a nation tranquility and trust in the wake of war, corruption and change is greatness. In any event, the record of Calvin Coolidge's Presidency, moored on devotion to the rule of law, provides wisdom worth retrieving today.

Russell Fowler, J.D., is Associate Director of Legal Aid of East Tennessee and Adjunct Professor of Political Science at the University of Tennessee at Chattanooga. He has written over 40 articles on law and legal history — a number of them on Calvin Coolidge — for the American Bar Association, Smithsonian Institution, *The Journal of Supreme Court History*, *The New England Law Review*, and others.

Presenting the Congressional Medal of Honor to Torpedoman Second Class Henry Breault for his actions while serving aboard the US Submarine O-5, March 8, 1924.

HE LED WITH
INTEGRITY

By Michael Dukakis

"Nobody ever questioned Coolidge's integrity, including his political opponents. And it is why Coolidge not only matters today, but is relevant for the times."

A decade after I campaigned for the highest office in the nation, I was asked to write an essay on Calvin Coolidge for the 1998 Coolidge Symposium at the John F. Kennedy Library. At the time, the main connection between us was that we each held the position of Governor of Massachusetts. Of course, he was also President. Other than that, I knew little about him. To a degree I assumed the stereotypical version of him — as a quiet, do-nothing President who neither accomplished nor aspired to much — was correct.

Once I researched Coolidge, I came away with an extraordinarily different take on the man. I found that he wasn't a conservative ideologue. In fact, this was a man, regardless of his political affiliation and conservative philosophy, who was guided first by what he thought was right for Americans. That was also a reflection of his unquestioned integrity and morality. Nobody ever questioned Coolidge's integrity, including his political opponents. And it is why Coolidge not only matters today, but is relevant for the times.

Among the things I discovered was, for example, that, when he ran for Lieutenant Governor in 1916, he and his gubernatorial running mate had proposed

Saluting historic aviator Charles A. Lindbergh (at podium) during a gala reception at the Washington Monument, June 11, 1927.

universal health care in Massachusetts. It was but one example of his long public record of compassion for people.

Coolidge was no enemy of labor. In fact, he stuck up for the little guy. Labor unions trusted and liked him. When he was asked to mediate the rancorous IWW strike in Lawrence in 1913, he almost single-handedly settled it by forcing mill owners to pay an extra twenty-five cents per hour to workers. Who would have thought that Coolidge had the determination and resolve to aggressively negotiate with the mill owners to pay their workers, which led to a settlement?

During the Boston Police strike of 1919, Coolidge was reluctant to make aggressive moves against the police union if there was some possibility of a settlement. In the end, however, he had to make some tough decisions. He did what any governor would have done under the circumstances — he fired the striking officers in the interest of public safety. At the time he thought it meant the end of his political career, but, in one of history's great ironies, it not only won him a huge majority in his final campaign for Governor, it was directly responsible for his selection as the Republican nominee for the Vice Presidency and his ultimate ascension to the Presidency.

Massachusetts Democrats liked and respected Coolidge. He reached out to them and independents during his long career in state politics. He sought out the leaders of organized labor and won their support. He carried that support into the state legislature where he developed remarkably close relationships with his Irish Democratic colleagues. "Calvin Coolidge can have anything he wants from me ... Cal's my kind of guy" said Jim Timilty, the Democratic boss of Roxbury and a colleague of Coolidge's in the Senate, as quoted in *Coolidge: An American Enigma*, by Robert Sobel.

Part of that sentiment dates from his work in his own district. Much of it, however, undoubtedly developed out of long and continued exposure to the electorate generally, literally hundreds of speeches in his statewide campaigns, and a sense on the part of average working citizens and their families that Coolidge was honest, decent, and understood and cared about them. He was, after all, a man who came from modest means and never forgot it, and people sensed it.

He believed strongly in grass roots organizing. He did an enormous amount of organizing himself, and, in fact, he'd make twelve to fifteen speeches a day during a campaign. You don't campaign the way Coolidge campaigned unless you like people, enjoy the political process, and believe deeply in what you are doing.

You don't think of Coolidge as a grass roots politician. But he was out climbing three-decker apartment buildings in Northampton and ringing the doorbells of those mostly Irish Roman Catholic working class folks who revered him, which led to his election to the City Council. This man was out in the community all the time. You learn a lot on those doorsteps and in those flats. "Only the man of broad and deep understanding of his fellow man can meet with much success in politics," Coolidge said, as quoted in *A Puritan in Babylon*, by William Allen White.

Coolidge was no socialist. But he was no moss-backed reactionary either. His political philosophy and the issues he championed were powerfully influenced by the Progressive movement of his time. In fact, he himself argued that no political party in America could remain viable "that wasn't progressive." He supported a shorter work week, maximum hours legislation for women and children, worker's compensation, the minimum wage, pensions for firefighters and their families, and a state income tax.

As Lieutenant Governor, he lambasted the Democrats for cutting appropriations for the state's mental hospitals. "Our party," he said, "will have no part in a

Presenting the Congressional Medal of Honor to Rear Admiral Thomas John Ryan, Jr., for his actions while in Yokohama, Japan during the 1923 Great Kanto earthquake, March 15, 1924.

scheme of economy which adds to the misery of the wards of the commonwealth — the sick, the insane and the unfortunate — those who are too weak even to protest."

Nor did he seem to be moderating his views as he took over the Governor's office in 1919. He asked for an increase in teacher salaries. He proposed and signed legislation imposing limits on a landlord's right to raise rents in the immediate post World War period. He wanted medical care for the indigent and a forty-eight hour work week, the latter over the strong opposition of the textile industry. He even proposed legislation authorizing employee representation on corporate boards, a radical proposal by any standard, particularly in those years.

In addition to these matters, his fight against child labor, prohibition, his support of women's suffrage and many other issues made him one of the most influential drivers of progressive reforms of the twentieth century.

A radically different take on Coolidge's accepted profile.

In his private life, the perks of office were meaningless. He lived frugally and didn't appear to have any interest in amassing wealth. Even though he held the highest offices at the state and national level, you don't get any sense that it turned his head. He campaigned as simply as he lived. In fact, he and I may be the only two Massachusetts Governors who used public transportation regularly. He didn't like entourages and was uncomfortable with ceremonial displays.

Lastly, his definition of the public interest still stands as one of the most eloquent ever delivered under the State House dome:

"The Commonwealth is one. We are all members of one body. The welfare of the weakest and the welfare of the most powerful are inseparably bound together. Industry cannot flourish if labor languishes. Transportation cannot prosper if manufactures decline. The general welfare cannot be provided for in any one act, but it is well to remember that the benefit of one is the benefit of all, and the neglect of one is the neglect of all.

"Do the day's work. If it be to protect the rights of the weak, whoever objects, do it. If it be to help a powerful corporation better to serve the people, whatever the opposition, do that. Expect to be called a stand-patter, but don't be a stand-patter. Expect to be called a demagogue, but don't be a demagogue.

"We need a broader, firmer, deeper faith in the people — a faith that men desire to do right, that the Commonwealth is founded upon a righteousness which will endure."

It was a pleasant accident that I got myself into this. Discovering Calvin Coolidge was a great experience, as was learning why he still matters today.

Michael Dukakis is a former legislator and Governor of the Commonwealth of Massachusetts, and was the Democratic Party's nominee for the U.S. Presidency in 1988. He is an attorney and a member of the Massachusetts Bar, and served four terms in the Massachusetts House of Representatives. He also served on the board of directors for Amtrak and became a professor of political science at Northeastern University, a visiting professor at Loyola Marymount University, and a visiting professor at UCLA.

With C. Bascom Slemp (second from right) as Slemp takes the oath to be the Secretary to the President, Sept. 4, 1923.

FIRST YEAR IN THE OVAL OFFICE

By Robert E. Gilbert

"Coolidge's successes with Congress reflected high levels of political acumen and hard work."

After midnight on August 3, 1923, Calvin Coolidge was awakened by his father in Plymouth Notch, Vermont, with the news that President Warren Harding was dead. After checking the Constitution to determine whether the Vice Presidential oath was sufficient or whether a new oath was necessary, he decided that, despite constitutional ambiguities, another oath *was* needed. He decided, too, that his father, a Notary Public, should administer it.

At 2:47 a.m., John Coolidge administered the oath, the first time ever that a father had sworn his son into the U.S. Presidency. The ceremony took place before a very small audience — the new First Lady, a Vermont Congressman, Coolidge's stenographer, his chauffeur, and a reporter — and in a room that he described as being filled with "sacred memories."

The image of Coolidge's oath-taking ceremony captured the public imagination. The "homestead inaugural" was highlighted often by the press and brought him considerable praise for its uniqueness and simplicity. It also suggested to the country that even though he was part of the scandal-scarred Harding administration, Calvin

Addressing the graduating class of 1924 at Howard University, June 6, 1924.

Coolidge emphasized character and would walk the path of righteousness.

To the new President's surprise, however, both the Attorney General and the Solicitor General were convinced that the swearing in by his father was not legally permissible. His father was a local official and simply did not have the authority to swear in federal officials. It was arranged, therefore, that the Presidential oath would be administered in the nation's capital by Justice A. A. Hoehling of the Supreme Court of the District of Columbia. Hoehling was asked never to mention this "ceremony" and no announcement of it was made for many years. This ensured that the appealing image of the "homestead inaugural" was never damaged during Coolidge's term and even lingers today.

Throughout the transition, Coolidge was anxious to exert his new authority. Even before he had left Vermont, he informed the Secretary of State that he wanted to meet with him immediately after his arrival in Washington. When he reached the capital, the President was so anxious to communicate to the country that the government was functioning and that a new leader was in place that he posed at his desk for photographers. Earlier, he had surprised General Pershing by giving him detailed instructions about Harding's funeral. No wonder that, by mid-month, Senator Henry Cabot Lodge was congratulating him for his "success so far which seems to me marked" and for making "a most excellent impression on the country." On August 28, Frank Stearns, Coolidge's close friend, commented, "It is interesting to see the President after he had been on duty five minutes. No one seeing him would have supposed he had not been there fifty years in the same place. Everything he said took the form of orders."

One order that Coolidge gave quickly was that after more than two years of Harding's "relaxed" ways, dignity and decorum had to be restored to the White

House. He instructed the chief usher, Ike Hoover, that he no longer wanted the public in the family rooms on the second floor as Harding had allowed, and remarked that "I want things as they used to be before." Theodore Roosevelt's daughter, Alice Roosevelt Longworth, commented after her first visit to the White House since the Coolidges moved in, "The atmosphere was as different as a New England front parlor is from a back room in a speakeasy."

Soon after becoming President, Coolidge asked House Speaker Frederick Gillette and Senate Majority Whip Charles Curtis for suggestions on a personal secretary who understood the political aspects of the President's office and who had familiarity with Congress and its members. Following this meeting, Coolidge chose former Republican Congressman Bascom Slemp of Virginia to fill the position.

With Slemp's help, Coolidge functioned smoothly as chief executive. The chief usher at the White House commented that, whereas Harding never liked details and was overwhelmed by them, Coolidge "takes it all in and understands it promptly." Reporters remarked that his desk invariably was neat and clean, not cluttered as Harding's had been. The new President held his first official cabinet meeting within two weeks of Harding's death, telling Cabinet members to "close ranks and let's go on."

In addition to his regular secretarial duties, Slemp functioned as something of a Presidential press secretary. Coolidge keenly understood the importance of the news media. At the outset, he promised to meet with the press on Tuesdays and Fridays, telling reporters, "I rather look forward with pleasure to having you come in twice a week, in order that I may talk to you, give you a little of the idea I may have of what the government is trying to do, and satisfy you, insofar as I can, on the questions that you ask." Questions, however, had to be submitted at least 10 minutes before the conference and the President determined which ones to answer. Sometimes he would allow spontaneous questioning but generally frowned on it. Although reporters were not permitted to quote the President directly or indirectly and had to attribute what he said to a "White House spokesman," they usually found Coolidge's remarks to be highly informative.

Meeting formally with them for the first time, Coolidge announced, "I want you to know the executive offices always will be open as far as possible so that you may get any information your readers may be interested to have. This is your government. You can be very helpful in the administration of it."

The President tightly stage-managed his interactions with the press. If he did not like the submitted questions, he would not answer them. At one conference, he appreciated none of the questions and simply said, "I have no questions today." At another, he joked, "I have a great many questions today but a great many I find are duplicates, triplicates and other cates." Coolidge was so anxious to befriend reporters that, in March 1924, he asked them a surprising favor: "I sometimes sit here at my desk and wish that I had the information at my command that is represented by you men ... and that brings me to the suggestion that if any of you think of the right kind of man for the secretaryship of the Navy, and I am perfectly serious about this though it may seem offhand and a little unusual, I should be very grateful ... if you will drop me a line or give the name to Mr. Slemp."

Reporters learned quickly that Coolidge meant what he said. The person chosen to be the new Navy Secretary was suggested by a newspaper source. This undoubtedly increased the President's credibility with the working press. Coolidge contributed to the institutionalization of the Presidential press conference by becoming the first President to put his bi-weekly meetings with the press on a regularly scheduled basis and by handling them well.

He also used radio with great effect. The President told one Senator that "I am fortunate that I came in with the radio.... I have a good radio voice and now I can get my messages across to them without acquainting them with my lack of oratorical abilities." After one radio broadcast, he commented to a friend that "the transmission of the message was evidently a great success, judging from the word which has been received from all parts of the country."

Coolidge's first major challenge as President came early in his term. In late August, 1923, a strike threatened to disrupt the flow of coal. A proactive Coolidge called the chairman of the Coal Commission to the White House for urgent consultations. He also summoned the federal fuel director and the acting chairman of the Interstate Commerce Commission and discussed with them plans for the distribution of fuel in the event of a strike. On August 22, the *Washington Star* reported that the word that came from the White House was that "the people will not be permitted to suffer from lack of fuel and the President is determined to use every agency of the government to make good this promise."

When Pennsylvania Governor Gifford Pinchot offered to serve as mediator, Coolidge promptly agreed. A strike began on September 1 but was resolved within a week. Mines were reopened and workers received a ten percent salary increase and a multi-year contract.

The President also kept busy with other matters during the opening weeks of his Administration. Early on, he met with the leaders of the American Federation of Labor to discuss relevant issues. In mid-August, he conferred with the National Commander of the Disabled American Veterans and then announced that he supported legislation to aid the disabled veterans of World War I. Coolidge also talked with the president of the National Federation of Federal Employees, called members of the Shipping Board to his office in order to devise a plan for the future operation of the United States merchant marine, and directed his Secretary of Agriculture to thoroughly investigate the conditions of wheat farmers and then develop a practical and economically sound plan to aid them.

In the early stages of his Presidency, Coolidge worked so strenuously that his secretary moved to tighten his schedule so as to protect his health and energy. Under this

With his father, John Coolidge, on the White House Lawn.

new arrangement, the President's official day began at 8:30 a.m. For ninety minutes, he answered mail and perused the morning papers. Between 10 a.m. and 12:30 p.m., he met with scheduled visitors in ten- to fifteen-minute periods. The half hour before lunch was reserved for receptions with delegations and for shaking hands with the many persons who wished to meet him. Lunch lasted for approximately forty-five minutes, and, by 2 p.m., the President was back at his desk for more paperwork. His official day typically ended around 6 p.m. but occasionally there would be evening dinners and/or meetings with members of Congress or executive branch officials. Coolidge was consumed by his Presidential duties. Slemp found that he "concentrated more intensely than any man I have ever known. He was always thinking, thinking, thinking."

Coolidge faced formidable obstacles in dealing with Congress. Although Republicans narrowly controlled both Houses, they were divided into the Old Guard and Progressive camps. The Progressives — who railed against the "special interests" — occasionally supported the Democrats on both organizational and legislative matters. Also, a group of Midwestern and Southern Senators had formed the "farm bloc" in 1921 and exerted considerable influence across party lines. The sharp divisions in Congress did not prevent Coolidge from trying to build bridges to all factions. As the first President to have his official entertaining funded by the government, he initiated a program of White House breakfasts as a way of reaching out to members of Congress of all stripes, even the one Socialist House member. On these occasions, Coolidge could be both charming and amusing.

Not intended primarily for discussing business, these sessions were meant to develop, as Coolidge later wrote, "a spirit of good fellowship which was no doubt a helpful influence to the transaction of public business." Nevertheless, legislation often was the main item on the agenda. In March, 1924, for example, Coolidge invited ten Republican Senators to breakfast and discussed various bills with them. Two days later, he hosted eight Senators at breakfast and urged them to pass his domestic program quickly. Following these sessions, the press reported that, "the Senate Finance Committee has been working day and night to report out the tax bill." The President told reporters, "I expressed to (the Senators) that they do what they could to expedite legislation. I received a report from Senator Smoot that they expected to be able to report the tax bill tomorrow or Monday.... I like to keep in touch, of course, with the members of the House and Senate. They are very busy men and unless I call them in considerable numbers at one time, I don't have the chance to keep up that contact that I would like to keep."

In addition to social gatherings, the President flattered, coaxed and used the prestige of his office to secure passage of his program. In December 1923, he wrote effusively to the House Speaker, sending him "congratulations and sincere personal appreciation for the altogether fine leadership you displayed during the organization of the House and of the Rules Committee. Your notable achievement in these matters augurs well for a most successful session." Around the same time, he asked each Republican Senator for suggestions on administrative appointments. Coolidge frequently invited individual members of Congress to meet with him at the White House for private discussions and/or to send him advice on policies. He invited them as well for cruises on the Presidential yacht, *The Mayflower*. Such invitations went to members of all political leanings and, occasionally, were extraordinary. When the wife of farm bloc leader Senator Arthur Capper died, Coolidge invited him to live at the White House for a time. The President even tried to cultivate his old Massachusetts rival, Senator Lodge, by sending him seventy-four roses on his seventy-fourth birthday. Also, he flattered Lodge by calling him often to the White House.

The likely pinnacle of Coolidge's first year as President came on December 6, 1923, when he delivered in person his first Annual Message to Congress. This was the first Presidential address in history to be broadcast on radio. Coolidge prepared painstakingly by making "an extensive survey of the various Departments" so that he would know them well and by consulting with a wide range of individuals.

Coolidge spoke to Congress for little over an hour and made some forty legislative requests in direct and forthright language. He urged establishment of a Permanent

Greeting labor leaders Dan G. Smith (second from right) and T.V. O'Connor (right), circa 1924.

Court of International Justice, a decrease in taxation on earned incomes, the elimination of nuisance taxes, the enactment of oil slick laws, an adjustment of the foreign debt, the creation of a new reforestation policy, the expansion of the civil service system, the abolition by Constitutional amendment of the right to issue tax-free securities, and the resumption of the opening of intercoastal waterways. He also recommended that Congress establish a separate cabinet level department of education and welfare, provide expanded health services for veterans, appropriate funds for medical courses at Howard University, set up reformatories for women and young men serving their first prison sentence, and enact a Constitutional amendment limiting child labor.

Concerned about the strength of the military and the viability of the Coast Guard, the President recommended that the Army be enlarged, that new submarines be authorized for the Navy and that power boats be supplied to the Coast Guard. Further, he recommended that the United States foreign service be reorganized, indicated his willingness to "go to the economic and moral rescue of Russia" provided that the Russian regime respected "the sanctity of international obligations," and reminded his audience that while the Monroe Doctrine must be maintained, "our duty now is to give stability to the world."

Without doubt, Coolidge's first message to Congress was that of a strong, activist chief executive urging an extensive agenda on the legislature. It suggested that the President was comfortable in his new role and fully embraced his responsibilities as legislative leader.

Coolidge did not get everything he wanted from Congress just as no President does. Nevertheless, by the time Congress adjourned in June, 1924, it had largely approved an impressive number of Coolidge's proposals. It reorganized the foreign service, decreased taxes on earned incomes, repealed many nuisance taxes and authorized more than $12 million for additional Coast Guard motor boats. It also prohibited the spreading of oil or oil refuse by vessels in U.S. territorial waters, authorized the expenditure of $6.8 million for additional hospital facilities for veterans, approved the establishment of independent reformatories for women and young men, and provided a new policy on reforestation. In June, 1924, Congress also approved a Constitutional amendment limiting child labor, but it was not ratified by two-thirds of the states.

Besides these legislative victories, Coolidge succeeded in protecting the executive branch from Congressional encroachments. These centered on the Harding Administration scandals that had reached a crescendo during Coolidge's early Presidency. The Senate appointed an investigating committee to look into the matters, particularly the activities of Interior Secretary Albert Fall and Navy Secretary Edwin Denby. Unwilling to be pushed into precipitous action, Coolidge remained calm and cautious. In late January, he indicated that he had instructed the Justice Department to observe the Senate hearings and to be prepared to take legal action if criminality was uncovered. A few days later, however, he announced that he had decided to appoint a two-person committee, composed of a Democrat and a Republican, to investigate and prosecute all wrongdoing.

On February 11, 1924, the Senate challenged the President directly by passing a resolution instructing him to fire Navy Secretary Denby. Coolidge responded firmly: "No official recognition can be given to the passage of the Senate Resolution…. The President is responsible to the people for his conduct relative to the retention or dismissal of public officials. I assume that responsibility." He then went on to remind the Senate that except for impeachment, "the dismissal of an officer of the government … is exclusively an executive function." Within days, however, Denby resigned and Coolidge accepted his resignation "with regret." Around this time, former President Taft praised the President for the "quickness with which he acts, the hardheadedness that he displays and the confidence that he is stirring in the people."

By repudiating Senate Resolutions that he saw as unconstitutional, Coolidge safeguarded the executive branch from legislative domination. By strongly supporting his own two-person investigating committee, he diverted public attention from Congress, communicated that he would not tolerate impropriety and greatly lessened corruption as an issue in the 1924 campaign. Coolidge's successes with Congress reflected high levels of political acumen and hard work.

———————————

During his first year, Coolidge also enjoyed a number of international successes. Mexico had long objected to the exploitation of its oil reserves by American corporations and the issue had become dangerously contentious. Diplomatic relations between the two countries had been severed and recognition of the Mexican government withdrawn. Following intensive negotiations between the United States and Mexico leading to the Bucareli Agreement, the United States agreed to accept Mexican control of subsoil minerals with the understanding that regulatory activity by Mexico would not be made retroactive past May 1, 1917.

When Coolidge met at the White House with the American negotiators, they informed him that the government of Mexico approved it and outlined its implications for the United States. According to press reports, at least two weeks would be required for the President and State Department to study the Agreement in order to determine whether it adequately protected American interests. However, within a week, Coolidge wrote to both negotiators and congratulated them on their ''fine piece of work'' and their success in resolving the long-standing problems with Mexico.

The President then recognized Alvaro Obregon as President of Mexico and restored diplomatic relations with a country he referred to as "our sister Republic." When rebels tried to overthrow the Obregon regime a few months later, Coolidge provided weapons, ammunition and aircraft to stop them. Within three months, the Mexican government crushed the rebellion. Coolidge further strengthened U.S.-Mexican relations when he announced that the United States would be a good neighbor to Mexico and would respect Mexican sovereignty.

Coolidge continued his diplomatic success by achieving Senatorial consent to ratify numerous treaties. At the end of the 1924 Congressional session, Senator Lodge, Chairman of the Senate Foreign Relations Committee, wrote the President about his "remarkable achievements in foreign affairs." He pointed out, "in the one session of Congress which we have had since you became President, we have reported to the Senate and ratified thirty-two treaties. No such record ... has ever been made by any administration. That in itself is complete proof of the great activity and energy shown by your administration from the day when you took the reins of power."

During his first year as President of the United States, Calvin Coolidge was a hard-working, competent and productive chief executive. The press reported that he was almost constantly at his desk, even working on Sundays. Coolidge's heavy schedule reflected not only his lifelong work ethic and the demanding nature of the Presidency but also his real enjoyment of the office. Being President gave him great satisfaction.

On December 7, 1923, Coolidge announced that he was a candidate for the 1924 Republican presidential nomination. The new President sought election to a term in his own right and was a shrewd strategist. Rival after rival fell.

By mid-April, the President had amassed almost all of the delegate votes needed for victory. Former President Taft commented that "I don't remember a case in which a party is so dependent on a man." On June 12, Coolidge swept to a landslide victory at the Republican Convention where ninety-six percent of delegates supported him. The Convention then nominated former Illinois Governor Lowden for Vice President, but he, apparently convinced

With members of the White House Photographer's Association.

that the Harding-era scandals would defeat Republicans, shocked the delegates by declining the nomination. Budget Director Charles Dawes was then nominated and joined the ticket.

The Republican National Convention was an enormous victory for Coolidge. The platform followed the President's wishes in all respects; his major rivals had been crushed. He was now the undisputed leader of the Republican Party and its candidate for the Presidency. This was surely the greatest moment of political triumph in Calvin Coolidge's life. Soon, however, he would be grief-stricken.

Just twenty-five days after Calvin Coolidge's overwhelming nomination for president, his sixteen-year-old son and namesake, Calvin Jr., died of blood poisoning. The President of the United States was devastated. Coolidge blamed his political ambitions for his son's death, writing that if he had not been President, young Calvin would "not have raised a blister on his toe, which resulted in blood poisoning, playing lawn tennis on the South Grounds." He also complained that he lacked the power to save the boy and commented very revealingly that, when young Calvin died, "the power and the glory of the Presidency went with him."

Although unfamiliar at the time with clinical depression, those close to President Coolidge recognized that something profound had taken place in his life. His wife said that after Calvin Jr. died, Calvin Sr. had "lost his zest for living"; his surviving son, John, remarked that "my father was never the same again after my brother died." Coolidge's White House physician described the President as "temperamentally deranged" and his secretary found him to be "mentally ill." The chief usher at the White House remarked that all who came into contact with Coolidge knew that he was "highly disturbed."

Calvin Coolidge's first eleven months as President were marked by astuteness and achievement. He greatly impressed the press, worked hard to cultivate Congress, succeeded in securing passage of much of his progressive legislative agenda, distanced himself from the Harding-era scandals, projected integrity to the nation, showed skill and boldness in foreign policy, and emerged as the unchallenged leader of the Republican Party. When his son died, however, Coolidge succumbed to clinical depression — for which no medications were then available — and largely withdrew from politics and the Presidency. He was a sick and disabled leader after July, 1924, despite his earlier effectiveness.

This was the tragedy of Calvin Coolidge.

Robert E. Gilbert, Ph.D., is the Edward W. Brooke Professor of Political Science at Northeastern University and a specialist on the American presidency. His articles have appeared in such journals as *Presidential Studies Quarterly, Political Psychology, Politics and the Life Sciences* and *Congress and the Presidency*. His books include *The Mortal Presidency: Illness and Anguish in the White House, Managing Crisis: Presidential Disability and the 25th Amendment* and *The Tormented President: Calvin Coolidge, Death and Clinical Depression*.

On the farm at Plymouth Notch, undated.

An Honest Public Servant

By Jerry L. Wallace

"President Coolidge gave the American people, as Will Rogers observed, the kind of government they wanted; that is, honest, efficient, economical, and pro-growth."

Regardless of the political office he held at the moment, Calvin Coolidge never lost sight of himself as a private citizen — *Mr.* Coolidge — who would one day return to his hometown to live among his friends and neighbors. In short, unlike so many of his colleagues, he never became addicted to the political world about him and its peculiar lifestyle. This ability to walk away from it all, so to speak, had its advantages. Throughout his political career, it gave him a certain degree of independence in approaching the issues of the day and permitted him, when he believed it necessary, to take difficult, unpopular stands. Notably, in the summer of 1927, it allowed him to do the unheard of: renounce a second full Presidential term by choosing not to run again in 1928. Then, when his work in Washington was done, he put aside the power and the glory of the Presidency, packed his grip, and returned without regret to Northampton and his duplex home, where he was again one with the people.

He insisted on respect for the office he held. Even when they dined alone in the State Dining Room of the White House, the President and the First Lady

At Plymouth Notch with son, Calvin, and father, John Coolidge, undated.

dressed formally; and if a family member was to join them, as son John once learned, he, too, was expected to dress for the occasion, for he dined with the President of the United States. On the other hand, on his birthday, as Mr. Coolidge rather than Mr. President, he could dress up in cowboy gear, a gift to him from Boy Scouts, and, as he said, give the folks a laugh. After his retirement from politics, he rejected employment offers from companies wanting to exploit his status as a former President rather than to hire him for what he had to offer. He eventually became a director of the New York Life Insurance Company, which suited him well, as he was a strong exponent of life insurance for the prudent protection it offered young families and the savings it accumulated for old age.

In his long political career — beginning on December 6, 1898, with his election to the Northampton City Council, and ending with his retirement from the Presidency on March 4, 1929 — Coolidge was a politician very much in tune with his times. No stiff ideologue was he. He had a sympathetic and understanding view of people and their concerns and needs. Within the confines of his moderate conservative philosophy, he was flexible and accommodative. This is best seen in his many years in politics in Massachusetts, then a leading industrial state and noted for its progressive spirit. Here, he stands out as an engaged, constructive, forward-looking official. The following is taken from his inaugural address as Governor, January 2, 1919: "Let there be a purpose in all your legislation to recognize the right of man to be well born, well nurtured, well educated, well employed, and well paid."

As President, Coolidge found Washington to be a different world with different demands than Boston. Presiding over the federal establishment, governed by the Constitution, he was responsible for fulfilling the commitments made to the people in the 1920 and 1924 Republican campaigns. Consequently, his Administration emphasized policies returning the federal government to a peacetime basis, stimulating economic growth and development, and, on the international front, assisting Europe to recover from the trauma of the Great War and encouraging efforts for world peace. His domestic fiscal priorities often put him in the role of restraining government growth — a Horatio at the Gate — which he did by fully exercising the new powers given him under the Budget and Accounting Act of 1921. To put it bluntly, it was the kind of government that emphasized "making every dollar sweat," as his Budget Director put it so well.

While popular with the public for the deficit reductions, tax cuts and economic growth it brought, the President's program of constructive economy made him few friends among Washington's politicos and bureaucrats. Indeed, bureaucrats, with their narrow focus on agency initiatives, complained about the lack of funding for what they perceived to be their worthy projects. The old line Theodore Roosevelt and Wilson progressives, who favored an activist and expanding federal government, were disillusioned too by the President's tight-fisted, minimalist approach to governing. They joined with those who, seeing Coolidge as Bay State interloper, never accepted him into Washington's official circles. In implementing his program, the President bypassed such opponents and malcontents by skillfully using the new technology of radio to go directly to the people and garner their support. He also was careful to maintain good relations with newspaper reporters and their associates, the photographers and newsreel men.

President Coolidge gave the American people, as Will Rogers observed, the kind of government they wanted; that is, honest, efficient, economical, and pro-growth. It was also a government that, with the exception of Prohibition enforcement, minded its own business, leaving citizens free to follow their own light. At the end of his Presidency, he retired more popular than when he entered office — an honor few Presidents hold — and if he had so chosen, the American people would have gladly rewarded him with another Presidential term. One test of a successful politician in a democracy is giving the people the government they want. In this, Coolidge was surely a success.

Historically speaking, President Coolidge presided over a time of social and political transition in American life: the old order was passing while another was taking form. There are clear indications that he had an inkling of this. Near the end of his Presidency, Coolidge noted that perhaps the times now called for someone — he was probably thinking of Herbert Hoover — who knew how to spend money, rather than save it, like himself. Indeed, his Administration had been moving in that direction. This is seen, for instance, in the $275 million plans for the Federal Triangle in Washington, which would transform the place into a modern city, as well as for new federal buildings scattered about the country. Then, again, shortly before his death in early January 1933, and only weeks before the inauguration of Franklin D. Roosevelt, he confessed to a friend that he no longer fitted in with the times. He recognized, it seems, that momentous changes were in the works. It is rare, of course, for a politician to have this understanding of his time and place and the power to recognize and accept that his moment on the political stage had come and gone.

Coolidge's philosophy of government was based primarily on a nineteenth century point of view, harkening back to the days of Cleveland and McKinley when he was a young man. For him, the bedrock of democratic government rested at the state and local level, where citizens came together to build a pleasing democratic commonwealth. Throughout his Presidency, his theme was that what was needed was "not more Federal Government, but better local government." In his mind, there was always before him the example of Massachusetts, one of the nation's most impressive and progressive states early in the twentieth century. Coolidge with his Massachusetts experience looked down at times with condescension upon the federal establishment and its ways. An example of this is seen, for instance, in his comments in his *Autobiography* that the Massachusetts inaugural ceremonies were "more ceremonious than the swearing-in of a President at Washington." In the case of the latter, he "was struck by the lack of order and formality that prevailed." (The Congress, let it be noted, was responsible for staging the inaugural ceremonies.)

On several occasions, as President, he would call on states to fulfill their governing responsibilities, rather than allow the federal government to encroach upon their rights. Their weakening status within the federal system troubled him deeply. He did what he could to stop this erosion of their power, but, frankly, few rallied to this effort. It was almost as though no one was listening. Indeed, the states themselves when offered federal dollars for highway building or flood control or whatever were only too eager to accept them. It should be emphasized here that the President did not view the doctrine of state rights as "a privilege to continue in wrong-doing but as a privilege to be free from interference in well-doing."

The Great Depression and World War II would suddenly and unexpectedly overwhelm his Jeffersonian view of the primary role of state and local government. It passed into history with his generation. The generally accepted concept of a limited and distant federal government of Coolidge's day was replaced by "Big Government," overseen by a President vastly more powerful and influential than he, and who served, moreover, as the leader of the free world. The American people, who once resented government involvement in their lives and work, came to accept it as a necessity of the modern world in which they lived. Coolidge, of course, could never have envisioned such sweeping and profound changes. While he would not have welcomed them, given his worldview, we can speculate that he would have accepted them. For Coolidge did recognize the people's right in a democracy to have the kind of government they wished. The young Calvin Coolidge had learned that long ago in those Plymouth town meetings. He also knew that the world changes, bringing new demands and requiring adjustment to governmental institutions. As post-war Governor of Massachusetts, he himself had overseen many such changes. I suspect, too, that Coolidge realized, along with Jefferson, that in the end, the world belongs to the living generation.

Harvesting crops at Plymouth Notch, undated.

With members of his cabinet on the White House lawn, April 11, 1924.

As he climbed the political ladder, Coolidge never forgot or pushed aside those who helped him in his advancement. "A man ought to be loyal to those who have been loyal to him," he said. This abiding loyalty to his political friends, both high and low — U.S. Senator W. Murray Crane, his mentor, and Northampton shoemaker, Jim Lucey, also his mentor — mark him as a politician's politician. We are told that Coolidge's first act after sitting down at the Presidential desk was to write old Jim Lucey, telling him that he would not be at that desk without his past help. In his *Autobiography*, he wrote of Senator Crane, who had died in 1920, "What would I not have given to have had him by my side when I was President!" Coolidge was not a man to use the exclamation point indiscriminately, and this is the only instance of its use in his *Autobiography*.

When it came to doing the day's work, Coolidge was able to identify his goals, set priorities, and then develop strategies for achieving them. As President, he had two primary goals, each aimed at encouraging economic growth: first, reducing the public debt, bloated after the Great War; and second, lowering income tax rates. In both these areas, through his leadership and persistence, Coolidge was successful. The key to his success was in reducing government spending by putting government operations on a business footing. The debt was lopped off by five and a quarter billion dollars and there were three major reductions in taxes greatly reducing or eliminating altogether taxes for most individuals. Mention should be made of tariff stability as well, for it too was a major concern of the President, who believed the tariff to be the foundation of the nation's prosperity. Here, however, no action was required on his part, other than insisting that Congress not tamper with the existing Fordney-McCumber tariff, and Congress complied. Internationally, his Administration aimed at the restoration of European economies and the reconstruction of the international gold standard. Here, too, considerable progress was made by the end of his term. Adding another perspective on this matter, Coolidge observed, "The higher our standards (of living), the greater our progress, the more we do for the world."

In carrying out his duties, unlike many politicians, Coolidge did not attempt to skirt unpopular or difficult issues or tasks, which could cost him politically, by ignoring them or pushing them off onto others. Rather, once they arrived at his desk, he faced up to them, showing his political skills by handling them in such a way as to avoid political damage or even turning them to his advantage. A classic example of this was his reorganization and consolidation of the Massachusetts bureaucracy as Governor from one-hundred eighteen departments into eighteen.

He also demonstrated political courage on several occasions by "saying no" to popular legislation supported by powerful special interest groups. This led *TIME* magazine to describe him as the "No-Man." In May and June of the election year of 1924, for example, he vetoed the World War Soldiers' Bonus Bill, Bursum Pension Bill for veterans and widows of wars, 1812-1904, and the Postal Salary Increase Bill, all having sizable constituencies of supporters. The press characterized them as "economy vetoes." Rejecting the pleas of the Farm Bloc, he twice vetoed the McNary-Haugen Farm Bill, once in 1927 and again in 1928, another election year. In all instances, these vetoes were carried out in such a way that there was no significant harm for him or his party. Following the great Mississippi flood of 1927, the Congress proposed flood control legislation creating a new bureaucracy and proposing to spend an astonishing $1.4 billion. Coolidge faced a dilemma. On the one hand, he found the bill totally unacceptable: "[T]he most extortionate proposal ever made upon the nation's revenues," he said. Yet, legislation was needed and a veto of the bill might well be disastrous for his party in the coming election in 1928. The President chose to use firm persuasion with the Congress. It worked. The result was an acceptable bill that kept spending within a reasonable limit of $500 million, required state and local participation, and assigned the engineering task to the existing Army Corps of Engineers.

For Coolidge, politics was an art, and among his skills, he possessed an excellent sense of political timing. He knew when to act and when not to act, which is often key to political success and survival. He once said to Secretary of Commerce Hoover, "If you see ten troubles coming down the road, you can be sure that nine of them will run into a ditch before they reach you and you have to battle with only one of them."

Coolidge was a first rate executive, a master of picking and retaining good men and of delegating to them the day's work. A case in point is Dwight Morrow, who he sent as ambassador to Mexico with only one instruction: "Keep us out of war." Through his good work, friendly, outgoing attitude, and the aid of Charles A. Lindbergh, Morrow did succeed in putting right our relations with Mexico. Often overlooked, the President's appointments to the federal judiciary were notable for their high quality. This reflected, no doubt, his profound respect as a lawyer for the law and the bench. It is of interest to recall that his one appointee to the Supreme Court, Harlan Fiske Stone, who had been his Attorney General, was later raised to Chief Justice by no less than Franklin D. Roosevelt.

Few Presidents have used their Cabinet more effectively and successfully than Coolidge. He thought of his Cabinet secretaries as "his" and would commonly refer to them as "my Secretary of the Treasury" or "my Secretary of Commerce." Neither Hoover nor Andrew Mellon, both men of power, public standing, and great wealth, intimidated him. In his Administration, department heads actually ran their operations and did a good job of it. There were no scandals among them on his watch. He picked qualified men and then left them alone to do their jobs. Individually, they liked and respected him, although they might differ with him on occasion. He considered himself a coordinator, not a boss. In turn, he expected them to be fully answerable for their actions. While not involving himself in the day-to-day workings of the departments, through regular Cabinet meetings and frequent individual conferences, he made certain that his Cabinet officials knew what he wanted and expected of them. They developed policies, which he sometimes modified or occasionally disapproved, and oversaw programs.

An example would be the operating policies developed and put in place for the new, fast-growing radio industry by Secretary of Commerce Hoover, a challenging task that he handled well. When the press had questions concerning a department, they went to the appropriate Cabinet officer for an answer, not to the President. Coolidge's use of his Cabinet was based not only on his managerial style of delegation but also on his concern (reinforced, no doubt, by the Harding scandals) that the President be insulated from any departmental controversy or scandal. A Cabinet official, he pointed out, was replaceable — but the President had to stay. This approach, unfortunately, led to some historians concluding that Coolidge was not in charge. He was very much so. It was he who set the agenda and saw that it was carried through.

In sum, Calvin Coolidge was an honest, principled and capable politician in tune with his times. As an executive, he set goals and produced results. His forte was making government work efficiently, effectively and economically. As a legislator and executive, he stood for policies favored by the people. They in turn rewarded him by electing and re-electing him to various posts year after year. That is the acid test for any politician. Coolidge deserves to be honored and remembered as an exemplary public servant.

Jerry L. Wallace is a historian, writer and a retired archivist from the National Archives and Records Administration in Washington, D.C. He has been a member of the Calvin Coolidge Memorial Foundation since 1971 and is currently researching Calvin Coolidge and the 1920s. He served as historian/archivist of three Presidential inaugural committees in 1973, 1981, and 1985, and is now archivist at Southwestern College in Winfield, Kansas.

Laying the cornerstone of the George Washington Masonic National Memorial in Alexandria, Virginia, November 1, 1923.

HE REVERED THE
FOUNDERS

BY L. JOHN VAN TIL

"Indeed, the nation would be much better served if more of its Presidents had a world view as consistent as Coolidge's."

Consult almost any history or political science textbook of the past 50 years as it comments on the 1920s, and very likely it will portray Calvin Coolidge negatively, frequently referring to him as a dumb, indolent, anti-intellectual pawn of Big Business. In this view, Coolidge was a political accident who, upon becoming President of the United States on August 2, 1923, slept through his five-and-a-half-year Presidency. While he slept, say his critics, the nation drifted towards disaster — which came in the form of a gigantic stock market crash and great economic depression.

How did this apparent political naif, this so-called simpleton, this relic of the nineteenth century become President, *conventional* historians and political scientists ask in their best-selling texts. After penning a few lines of ridicule, most historians then pushed any serious consideration of President Coolidge off to the side and continued their speculation about what, in their opinion, "should have been" in the 1920s — that "lost" decade between Woodrow Wilson and Franklin D. Roosevelt.

Does Calvin Coolidge make any difference from today's point of view in America? Sadly, decades of hostile historical comment about Coolidge in hundreds of texts have left a large percentage of the American public with a decidedly negative image of him. It is the contention of this essay that Calvin Coolidge certainly should be appreciated for several reasons. First, the textbook image of him believed by most who have matriculated in the nation's schools is simply dead wrong. The prevailing view of him is not merely a matter of interpretation, it is a question of facts, and the texts have the facts wrong in most instances. Second, as I found in a several-years-long study of his writings, Coolidge was a very thoughtful man with a comprehensive view of the world. Indeed, the nation would be much better served if more of its Presidents had a world view as consistent as Coolidge's. We should strongly suggest that his writings be read today because they have a deep wisdom in them that was born of the man's basic common sense. Besides, he was a man of great humor and we all can use more of that.

Fortunately, a more balanced view of him may now emerge as a result of a modest Coolidge renaissance that is now under way. Evidence of this appears in several new scholarly biographies of him by leading historians, numerous conferences devoted to a further exploration of Coolidge and his era, and, not least of all, in a quirky political endorsement of him by a recent, very popular President. The last reference, of course, is to the now-famous White House scene in which Ronald Reagan, upon assuming office, ordered Coolidge's portrait to be hung in the Cabinet Room. Reporters snickered, and when their inquiries about it reached Reagan, he emphatically said that Coolidge was *his* kind of President because he cut government spending and lowered taxes — two things Reagan hoped to do.

British historian Paul Johnson also contributed to the Coolidge revival, especially in his thoughtful evaluation of Coolidge in his best-selling *Modern Times*. In fact, it was Johnson's view that encouraged me to find Coolidge's works and read them for myself. It was soon clear that they were not easily available and out of print since the 1920s. It occurred to me that a new edition of his main works would be valuable for the emerging Coolidge revival and for others interested in him and his era. I resolved to study and prepare a new edition of Coolidge's published works and then write an account of his intellectual development. Both of these projects are now complete. Two main things emerged from my study of his writings, one expected and the other not. Naturally, a better understanding of Coolidge flowed from this study. *On the other hand, to my surprise, it became evident that Calvin Coolidge was a very thoughtful man, a quality never implied or suggested by text writers and critics.* After reviewing several notebooks full of quotations gleaned from my study of his speeches and addresses, it was also evident that Coolidge's writings displayed a rather well-thought-out set of ideas about society, government, business, the nature of man, and related topics. Was it possible that the proverbial "Silent Cal" was also "Thinking Cal?" And, since Coolidge wrote all of his own speeches and addresses, they reflect his thought, not the thinking of speech writers as is often the case with subsequent Presidents.

Concluding that Coolidge was exceptionally thoughtful raised the question: How did he get that way? Did he read his way to a comprehensive world view? His personal library, preserved in the Forbes Library, Northampton, Massachusetts, suggests that he was, indeed, very widely read. The same message, in the form of copious literary quotations and paraphrases, jumps out of the pages of his dozens of essays and speeches. And, his extensive knowledge of history is everywhere present in his writings. Coolidge himself, however, tells us very clearly in his *Autobiography* from whence it was that he obtained his interest in the way the world works, that is, how he developed a coherent world view. It was, he says, his professors at Amherst who opened the door to a comprehensive view of life. Quoting a crucial passage from his *Autobiography* sums up his intellectual development very succinctly in his own words. After noting that he studied history and literature in his first years at Amherst, Coolidge focused on what to him was the critical point in his education: "It always seemed to me that all our other studies were in the nature of preparation for the course in philosophy. The head of the department was Charles E. Garman, who was one of the most remarkable men with whom I ever came in contact.... Beginning in the spring of the junior year, his course extended through four terms. The first part was devoted to psychology, in order to find out the capacity and the limits of the human mind.... We were not only learning about the human mind but learning how to use it, learning how to think.... The human mind has the power to weigh evidence, to distinguish between right and wrong and to know the truth. I should call this the central theme of his philosophy.... We looked upon Garman as a man who walked with God. His course was a demonstration of the existence of a personal God, of our power to know Him.... The conclusions which followed from this position were logical and inescapable. It sets man off in a separate kingdom from all other creatures in the universe, and makes him a true son of God and a partaker of the Divine nature.... He believed in the Bible and constantly quoted it to illustrate his position.... To Garman was given a power which took his class up into a high mountain of spiritual life and left them alone with God.... What he revealed to us of the nature of God and man will stand. Against it 'the gates of hell shall not prevail.' "

It seems remarkable, indeed, that all of this was still so clear in Coolidge's mind thirty-five years distant from the classroom at Amherst. No doubt, it is evidence of the strength of Garman's influence on the shaping of Coolidge's mind.

The power of Garman's influence is everywhere evident in Coolidge's two major works, *The Price of Freedom* and *Foundations of the Republic*, first published in 1924 and 1926 respectively. As noted, I have prepared a new edition of these works along with a one-hundred twenty-five-page essay which traces the development and structure of his thought. We turn now to a consideration of two principal characteristics of Coolidge's life and thought.

First, Coolidge had a systematic and comprehensive view of the world, one that was obviously and distinctively Christian. Second, he had supreme confidence in the societal and governmental principles the Founding Fathers hammered out for the new nation, in their own writings and in the Declaration of Independence and Constitution. These features of Coolidge's thought are woven into virtually every speech he delivered and essay he wrote.

Turning to the first theme, we may observe that many of Coolidge's contemporaries, Americans who came to maturity in the last quarter of the nineteenth century, would not be surprised to hear someone refer to Coolidge as having a Christian world view, because most of them thought of their own lives and world in the same way. Notwithstanding late twentieth century intellectuals' and Supreme Court Justices' views to the contrary, America into the 1920s was in many ways a Christian society. This congruence between Coolidge's view of America and many Americans' view of it was one of the reasons why Coolidge was the most popular public figure in America throughout the decade of the 1920s, even after he left office and was replaced by Hoover. Once out of office, he was paid a small fortune for articles he wrote for magazines and newspapers because the public wanted to know what Coolidge thought about any and every thing.

There was, however, something distinctive about Coolidge's Christian world view, rooted as it was in the teaching of his beloved professor, Charles Garman. We can only touch a few of the highlights of this view here. More of them may be found in the essay referred to above. Beyond the usual Christian assumptions about life — that God was sovereign, that He made man in his image to rule over the Creation, that man sinned and could be redeemed, that man had a duty as image-bearer to create civilizations, and more — Coolidge focused on societal structures and how they *ought* to work.

At a military ceremony, circa 1924.

He thought society had a natural balance among its several segments — family, business, religious institutions, labor, education, and the like. Significantly, following Professor Garman, Coolidge believed that this balance had been disrupted by business practices in the Industrial Revolution, especially since the Civil

Breaking ground on the site of Hamline M.E. Church in Washington, D.C., circa 1924.

War. Leaders of industry had obtained power a thousand times greater than any man had held in the days of craftsmen. The new Captains of Industry, as they were called, gained great wealth and power while others working as laborers lost almost all control over their own lives and labor. It was especially frightful, and immoral, to Coolidge that such workers had no outlet for their creativity — an image-bearing quality each worker should exercise either on the job or in some other realm, Coolidge argued.

It should be noted in passing that this focus by Coolidge on creativity as part of life was but one dimension of his continuous emphasis on the spiritual, immaterial and transcendent aspects of human nature. Indeed, he pondered this at length in another of what I have called his "big picture essays," this one entitled "The Things That Are Unseen." The concluding lines of that piece sum up very well the importance of the spiritual dimension of life that Coolidge believed was crucial in one's view of man. Said Coolidge: "We do not need more material development, we need more spiritual development. We do not need more intellectual power, we need more moral power. We do not need more knowledge, we need more character. We do not need more government, we need more culture. We do not need more law, we need more religion. We do not need more of the things that are seen, we need more of the things that are unseen."

Elsewhere Coolidge spoke and wrote at length about the need for character, moral power and religion. In addition, he was adamant about his claim that we do not need "more laws." What was needed, he said, was a much better enforcement of existing laws.

To return to the main point here, an accumulation of great power by the Captains of Industry, Coolidge did not merely refer to it in the abstract in his speeches and essays. He put flesh and blood on this claim, especially in his essay

"Theodore Roosevelt," delivered as an address in New York City, just weeks before he was inaugurated as Vice President. Though he thought the problem had been largely tamed by that time, 1920, he wanted to make his view clear about the imbalance that had developed after the Civil War, an imbalance that Roosevelt had largely corrected through his anti-trust efforts.

His remarks about Roosevelt provide an example of another of his "big picture" essays and addresses. Noteworthy, too, is the fact that a number of these essays were biographical. That was no accident, as the following quotation makes clear. He states here, as in many other biographical essays, that great men have been sent from time to time to aid civilizations' development in special ways. Stated Coolidge: "Great men are the ambassadors of Providence sent to reveal to their fellow men their unknown selves. To them is granted the power to call forth the best there is in those who come under their influence. Sometimes they have come as great captains, commanders of men, who have hewed out empires, sometimes as statesmen, ministering to the well-being of their country, sometimes as painters and poets, showing new realms of beauty, sometimes as philosophers and preachers, revealing to the race, "the way, the truth, and the life," but always as inspirers of noble action, translating high ideals into practical affairs of life. There is something about them better than anything they do or say. … They come and go, in part mystery, in part the simplest of all experience, the compelling influence of the truth. They leave no successor."

These remarks set the stage for the main point of this essay, that is, that Teddy Roosevelt was a God-given leader who corrected the economic imbalance that had developed in America since the Civil War. Of course, this is part of Coolidge's larger view of history, a view that may be termed Augustinian, with elements of a devotion to "manifest destiny" in it. In short, history was a development through stages and now in America the last stage was unfolding. His view, in these respects, was much like that of many other Americans in the late nineteenth and early twentieth century, though his focus on the "unseen" is more dramatic.

Coolidge's view of societal structures and the need to keep them in balance illustrates the scope of his considerable thinking about how institutions should relate to one another in a civilization. Indeed, it was the foundation of his policies while in government service. Significantly, he saw government as just another of society's institutions. To be sure it had specific duties, as is evident in his view of Roosevelt's use of governmental power to correct an imbalance in the economic sphere. Stated another way, in his view government was limited in its role just as religion and business were limited. We turn now to see how Coolidge developed his view of government.

A basic distinction for him in this matter was to be found between the terms *government* and *state*. *Government* for him and his generation meant the constitutional apparatus that provided for ruling or governing society: The separate branches provided for in the Constitution, limitations on the powers and duties of each, election processes, amending powers, and the like. *State* for Coolidge, and again for his generation, referred to the series of social relationships found among citizens — political parties, religious organizations (including churches), family, unions, business firms, fraternal organizations, and more.

Strange as it may seem to most twenty-first century minds, each of these institutions in the minds of early twentieth century Americans also had its own *government*: Churches had ecclesiastical governments; families had paternal governments; and so on with all societal institutions. Stated another way, the *government* in each realm applied the rules (laws) which regulated its realm and its realm only. These distinctions have been largely lost today as the federal government has usurped power and authority previously held by each. To emphasize, when Coolidge talked about *government* and its powers, he thought of it as *civil* government, *one not possessed with immediate authority over all societal realms*. In short, he understood, as did his contemporaries, that *civil* government was but one kind of government, one with limited powers to be sure. In this, as in many other intellectual matters discussed here, he reflects the thinking of his beloved mentor, Charles Garman.

Government, or Civil Government as Coolidge liked to call it, was that government created by the Constitution. And, it was limited in two ways in his view. First, by the Constitution itself because it was a document that enumerated the powers of the government it created. This feature was strengthened by the Ninth and Tenth Amendments, worth quoting here:

> Amendment IX (1791) — The enumeration in the Constitution, of certain rights, shall not be construed to deny or disparage others retained by the people.

> Amendment X (1791) — The powers not delegated to the United States by the Constitution, nor prohibited by it to the States, are reserved to the States respectively, or to the people.

In addition to the limitations on the Civil Government found in the Constitution and its Amendments, it was also limited, in Coolidge's view, by virtue of the fact that it was but one of many institutions in society. To emphasize, it stood among the others — business, family, churches, labor, etc., all together as part of the natural order of things. From another angle, it may be said that Civil Government was not a superior or supreme institution in society, in Coolidge's view. How different this view is from that held by most in American society today! Today most people expect and assume that the Civil Government is the FIRST resort in solving problems rather than the last one as Coolidge and his contemporaries believed. With this view of government as limited, Coolidge constantly worked to reduce government — which had expanded greatly during the World War I, as governments always do during wars.

Attending services at the First Congressional Church in Washington, D.C., August 5, 1923.

Harding had created the Bureau of the Budget just before his untimely death and Coolidge soon put teeth into the Bureau and gave it life as a tool to help in the control and reduction of government expenditures.

We must note in passing that Coolidge was not opposed to new programs as many of his critics suggest, nor was he a mindless Dickensian Scrooge who delighted in destroying programs to save money. He favored many new projects over the years, when they made economic sense. He pushed developments in transportation, for example, both water and surface. Moreover, he was among the first to see the bright future of air transportation.

And where did Coolidge get his view of limited government ultimately? In addition to what he found in the Constitution itself, he learned much from the Founders themselves. It is evident in his essays and speeches that he was an accomplished student of the Founders' lives and writings. He spoke and wrote about many of them, noting the unique contribution each made to the American System. It may be said with confidence, based upon his own writing and the contents of his library, that Coolidge was very likely as knowledgeable as any President about American history, and especially so when it came to the Founding Fathers. Significantly, he not only quotes them, but often he also refers to them as he did to Theodore Roosevelt, as "ambassadors of Providence."

Like Lincoln, Coolidge thought that the Declaration of Independence was, in a way, more important than the Constitution. At least, the latter was not possible without the former. This fascination with the Declaration is not only evident throughout his writings but especially clear in his address delivered on the one-hundred twenty-fifth anniversary of this document. Interestingly, at that time in American history, when July 4 fell on a Sunday, the celebration took place on the next day. So it was that Coolidge presented his remarks about the Declaration on July 5, 1926, in Philadelphia under the title "The Inspiration of the Declaration." Among other things, Coolidge stated that the annual celebration of the Declaration was not so much a time to "proclaim new theories and principles as it was a time to reaffirm and reestablish those old theories and principles which time and the unerring logic of events have demonstrated to be sound."

Something of Coolidge's power with the pen is evident in this address. He noted that people from other lands, as well as Americans, viewed Independence Hall as hallowed ground. Indeed, to him it seemed to be as important to many as the Holy Land — a sacred place. He went on to say: "In its main features the Declaration of Independence is a great spiritual document. It is a declaration not of material but of spiritual concepts. Equality, liberty, popular sovereignty, the rights of man — these are not elements which we can see and touch. These are ideals. They have their source and their roots in religious convictions. They belong to the unseen world. Unless the faith of the American people in these religious convictions (endures), the principles of our Declaration will perish. We can not continue to enjoy the result if we neglect and abandon the cause."

In this we see the close tie in his mind between the faith of the Founders and the principles of the Declaration. The large audience before him at Independence Hall that day in July, 1926, would have felt perfectly comfortable with his view of the Founders' faith and the Declaration.

Before concluding this essay, a point or two more should be made. First, it is good to emphasize that Coolidge's considerable thought-life had two principal features, two pillars as it were — a comprehensive world view rooted in the Christian philosophy of his beloved Amherst mentor, Charles Garman. Mrs. Coolidge noted that throughout their married life Coolidge always had two books on his bedside stand — Garman's *Letters, Lectures and Addresses. ...* and the Bible. The second pillar of Coolidge's thinking was, as pointed out here, a deep devotion to the Founding Fathers and their achievements in creating the American System, its substance being on display in the Declaration and the Constitution.

And, one more point. Being a quiet and modest man, Coolidge seldom referred to an achievement of which he was most proud. During his senior year at Amherst — he subsequently was graduated *magna cum laude* — Coolidge entered a *national* essay contest which was open to all seniors of America's colleges and universities. The topic was the causes of the American Revolution. The prize was a one-hundred fifty dollar gold piece — worth a lot of money at that time. The judges decided, weeks after graduations around the country, that Coolidge won. When notified, Coolidge characteristically said nothing, placing the medal on his desk in the law office where he had begun to study law. Days later, a senior partner, and fellow Amherst graduate, walked in and saw the medal, congratulating Coolidge. Coolidge, who later as a seasoned politician said of speech, "Be brief. Above all, be brief," responded merely, "Thank you." His great, though quiet pride in winning the national essay is evident in his book *Foundations of the Republic*. In it he included the prize essay as the last item in the collection. The prestige associated with this prize in 1895 would be similar to, if not greater than, the Rhodes Scholarships awarded today. An obvious point, too, is the fact that this prize essay is powerful evidence of the fact that Coolidge was already a gifted and thoughtful person at an early age.

Was Coolidge the anti-intellectual simpleton and dullard his critics have claimed? A sustained examination of his life and writings does not support such a claim. As a matter of fact, a sustained examination of the record strongly suggests the opposite. Students today would be better off studying his life and ideas rather than those of recent Presidents for, unlike them, he shows much wisdom about how to live a successful life as a public servant.

L. John Van Til, Ph.D., is a Visiting Fellow at Harvard and has taught at the University of Wisconsin, the University of Texas and at Grove City College in Western Pennsylvania. His main academic interest has been intellectual history, as evidenced by his *Liberty of Conscience: The History of a Puritan Idea*. He has produced several hundred reviews, articles, essays and chapters in assorted publications. A new edition of the writings of Calvin Coolidge will include his book-length essay "Thoughtful Calvin Coolidge."

Exiting the U.S. Capitol Building (undated)

Delivering his first message to Congress, circa 1923

A MAN OF
MODESTY

BY WARD CONNERLY

"Coolidge had enormous faith in the ability of the people to govern themselves."

Every four years Democrat and Republican candidates debate each other and audition for the job of President of the United States of America. As I have observed them over the years, I compare their words and promises to the life and values of Calvin Coolidge. I conclude that all Presidential candidates could benefit enormously from such a comparison and from the model that Coolidge offers for public life.

Not only could the candidates benefit from an understanding of "Silent Cal," but so can anyone intent on entering public service. Better yet, the words and thinking of Coolidge should be part of the menu of required reading for all high school students.

Born on the Fourth of July in 1872, Calvin Coolidge was America's thirtieth president. He was a remarkable man of the people, as captured by his confession that "I know very well what it means to awaken in the middle of the night and realize that the rent is coming due, wondering where the money is coming from with which to pay it." Such candor is rarely found among political figures.

Addressing the Wisconsin Convention of the American Legion in praise of the Kellogg pact on August 15, 1928.

Coolidge was a man of integrity who synchronized his personal life to coincide with his desire to remain free to follow his convictions without the influence of political considerations. He states: "I always made my living practicing law up to the time I became governor, without being dependent on any official salary. This left me free to make my own decisions in accordance with what I thought was the public good. We lived where we did that I might better serve the people."

The lessons that Coolidge teaches are not limited to elected officials and those who pursue public office; they have application to all individuals, regardless of the path that we pursue in life. For example, Coolidge had a strong work ethic: "But we do not choose our ancestors. When we come into the world the gate of gifts is closed behind us. We can do nothing about it. So far as each individual is concerned all he can do is take the abilities he has and make the most of them. His power over the past is gone. His power over the future depends on what he does with himself in the present. If he wishes to live and progress he must work.... Any reward that is worth having only comes to the industrious. The success which is made in any walk of life is measured almost exactly by the amount of hard work that is put into it."

While the life of Coolidge offers many traits worthy of emulation, there is one that, for me, stands out above all others, and that is his modesty and sense of perspective about his own accomplishments. Despite having served the public for thirty-one years in positions that ranged from a member of the Northampton Common Council in 1898 to President of his nation for a six-year period that ended in 1929, Coolidge did not attribute his success to his considerable talent. Rather, he believed that his many accomplishments resulted from hard work. In a very telling passage that clearly sums up Coolidge the man, he said, "My life had been slow and toilsome, with little about it that was brilliant, or spectacular, the result of persistent and painstaking work, which gave it a foundation that was solid."

Unlike many elected officials who consider themselves bigger than life itself, Coolidge considered himself a man of modest or mediocre talent who progressed as he did solely because of constant hard work. Few politicians of our time hold such a minimalist view of their abilities.

Calvin Coolidge was a Republican, but throughout his distinguished career, he reached across the partisan divide to enlist the support of Democrats to address the needs of the people. Coolidge had enormous faith in the ability of the people to govern themselves. The basis of his views about self-government rested in his belief in the Creator. For him, God was present in all elements of the universe. It was from the power of God that man derived his power to conduct the affairs of the people. It was this belief that "sets man off in a separate kingdom from all the other creatures in the universe, and makes him a true son of God and a partaker of the Divine nature."

Coolidge elaborates further on this "Divine nature" by describing it as "the warrant for his [man's] freedom and the demonstration of his equality. It does not assume all are equal in degree but all are equal in kind. On that precept rests a foundation for democracy that cannot be shaken. It justifies faith in the people.... In time of crisis my belief that people can know the truth, that when it is presented to them they must accept it, has saved me from many of the counsels of expediency. The spiritual nature of men has a power of its own that is manifest in every great emergency from Runnymede to Marston Moor, from the Declaration of Independence to the abolition of slavery."

On more than one occasion, I have also ignored the "counsels of expediency" and placed my faith in the ability of the people to make the right decisions. That faith has consistently been rewarded by an outcome of my pleasure. I vividly recall a campaign in the state of Michigan to end preferential treatment on the basis of race, sex, color, ethnicity and national origin in the venues of public employment, public education and public

President Warren G. Harding addresses the House of Representatives with Speaker of the House Frederick H. Gillett and Coolidge seated behind him, circa 1920.

contracting. Known as the "Michigan Civil Rights Initiative," our campaign was opposed by every conceivable segment of the Michigan civic and political establishment — Democrats, prominent Republicans, labor unions, churches, the automakers, race advocates, municipalities, and the incumbent governor, to name a few. Public opinion polls throughout the campaign predicted rejection of the simple proposition that all citizens of Michigan should be treated equally by their government. A well-financed, high-profile opposition campaign filled with scare tactics was waged by our opponents.

On Election Day in November 2006, the people of Michigan reaffirmed the teachings of Coolidge and passed the Michigan Civil Rights Initiative, against all odds, by the overwhelming vote of fifty-eight percent to forty-two percent. I did not know the teachings of Coolidge during that campaign, but I was influenced by my own belief that the foundation of democracy is grounded in faith in the people and the invisible hand of "Divine nature." Had I known more about Coolidge at the time, I would have been comforted by his words that "expediency as a working principle is bound to fail."

The optimism and belief in the goodness of his fellow man is a Coolidge trait that is so desperately needed today, as America confronts a host of problems, each with the potential to unravel the social fabric of our nation: "The only way I know to drive out evil from the country is by the constructive method of filling it with good. The country is better off tranquilly considering its blessings and merits, and earnestly striving to secure more of them, than it would be in nursing hostile bitterness about its deficiencies and faults." A hearty "amen" to the counsel of "Silent Cal."

Ward Connerly, author of *Creating Equal: My Fight Against Race Preferences*, is founder and chairman of the American Civil Rights Institute, a former member of the University of California Board of Regents and an advocate of equal opportunity for all Americans. Connerly is the recipient of the Patrick Henry Award (1995), the Ronald Reagan Award (1998) and the Racial Harmony Hall of Fame Award (2000). He has been profiled on "60 Minutes" and in *The New York Times*, *The Wall Street Journal* and *Newsweek* magazine, and has appeared on "The NewsHour with Jim Lehrer," "Crossfire," "Meet the Press," and "NBC Nightly News," among others.

With Vice President Charles Gates Dawes (undated)

Signing the 1926 Mellon Tax Bill at the White House, February 16, 1926.

HE VALUED COMMON SENSE

By Alvin S. Felzenberg

"Coolidge put a greater premium on common sense ('horse sense' in Coolidge-speak) than he did on what he learned in books and saw in the press."

In recent years, the reputation of Calvin Coolidge has undergone a renaissance. Influenced by wise cracks of the "chattering class" of his era and, put off, perhaps, by his caustic wit, historians had long dismissed Coolidge as a non-entity or a fool. Coolidge's resurrection began in 1981, when his fellow-tax cutter, Ronald Reagan, whom the café set also dismissed as an intellectual lightweight, hung "Silent Cal's" portrait in the White House Cabinet Room.

Reagan's gesture revived interest in Coolidge and led to a reassessment of his Presidency. Coolidge has been the subject of two conferences: one, in 1995, at the Library of Congress, which houses his Presidential papers, and the other, in 1998, at the John F. Kennedy Presidential Library. Coolidge has been the subject of at least three recent books, a book of quotations, and a growing number of scholarly and popular articles. His autobiography, once allowed to gather dust in the basements of many libraries, has gone through several new printings.

Can a blockbuster motion picture focusing on his life or a Coolidge profile on PBS's the "American Experience" be all that far off? While Coolidge aficionados will not

Addressing graduates of Georgetown University, circa 1924

be holding their breath in anticipation of such media extravaganzas, the mere suggestion of such projects no longer provokes the dismissive laughter and derision it would have during the first four decades after Coolidge left office.

Coolidge is being re-examined, in part, for some of the very reasons that cause historians to leave him off lists of "near great" or "above average" Presidents in periodic surveys of Presidential greatness. In both peace and war, Franklin D. Roosevelt turned the Presidency into the preeminent branch of the federal government and greatly expanded the role the federal government played in the lives of citizens. Until most recently, most historians took FDR as the standard against which they judged all Presidents. Viewed through this lens, Coolidge, who departed the oval office merely four years before FDR entered it, appeared to have more in common with his nineteenth-century predecessors such as Grover Cleveland and Benjamin Harrison, than with Harry Truman or Lyndon Johnson.

Recent scholarship about both Herbert Hoover and Franklin D. Roosevelt has cast Coolidge in a new light. Most economists now attribute the United States' recovery from the Great Depression in 1942 to war-related military spending and the related expansion of the money supply to finance large budget deficits, rather than to any of FDR's New Deal programs. Moreover, economists and historians have also regarded the economic policies the traditionally much-maligned Herbert Hoover followed to have been closer to those of Roosevelt than to those of Coolidge. This has made Coolidge appear as an interesting contrast both in his style of governance and in political philosophy to that of activists such as FDR and his more immediate successors, from whom contemporary liberalism takes its inspiration. Reagan, who sought nothing less than a complete change in direction from the one in which the nation had been headed when he took office was keenly aware of this.

Courses and textbooks on modern America habitually skip from Wilson's epochal battle with the Senate over ratification of the Versailles Treaty to the stock market crash of 1929, which transpired early in Hoover's ill-fated single term as President. This is a mistake. Coolidge was a very competent President. He read people very well and named outstanding administrators to major posts. He also exhibited a philosophy of government and of governance that had much to recommend it. Those who take the time to examine Coolidge's life and his record will find that he and his example have much to impart to contemporary audiences.

———————

Few Presidents understood the people they led better than Calvin Coolidge. His understanding and reflection of their concerns resulted from his repeated asking for their votes in the almost continuous campaigns he waged for elective office, especially in the opening decades of his political career. Of all the nation's Presidents, Coolidge held the most number of elected posts. He held public office, virtually without interruption, from 1897 through 1929.

Unlike Woodrow Wilson, whose first elective office was Governor of New Jersey, and Herbert Hoover, whose political career began with his campaign for President, Coolidge had risen through the ranks. Wilson and Hoover were both fifty-four when they took the plunge. Coolidge had been in his twenties. Unlike other Presidents, who also entered electoral politics at an early age, such as Lyndon Johnson, Richard Nixon and Bill Clinton, Coolidge had not aspired to the Presidency decades prior to his ascension to it. His lack of such ambitions, however, stemmed not from a lack of self-confidence. "I thought I could swing it," Coolidge said, when asked to recall his sentiments when informed that he had succeeded to the Presidency upon the death of Warren G. Harding.

Coolidge looked upon each office as his opportunity to do to the people's business. He worked hard to provide what he considered excellent service to his constituents. He showed an earnestness and a seriousness that commanded their respect. If he came across as "all business," he also "delivered."

In his thirty-two years in public service, Coolidge saw himself as a problem solver and not as an ideologue. Though more widely read than his detractors assumed, Coolidge put a greater premium on common sense ("horse sense" in Coolidge-speak) than he did on what he learned in books and saw in the press. He also took a jaundiced view of "experts," few of whom he found to be "entirely disinterested" (as they and their admirers often claimed). Coolidge formed his political views according to what "seemed" and "felt" right to him, based on his life experience.

Coolidge articulated his view of government in a speech after he was sworn in as President of the Massachusetts State Senate. He titled the speech "Have Faith in Massachusetts" and his message, later published in a book by the same name, must have surprised both conservatives and progressives of his day as much as they would in ours. In a poignant excerpt, he said: "Do the day's work. If it be to protect the rights of the weak, whoever objects, do it. If it is to help a powerful corporation better to serve the people, whatever the opposition, do that. Expect to be called a stand-patter, but do not be a stand-patter. Expect to be called a demagogue, but do not be a demagogue. Do not hesitate to be called as revolutionary as science. Do not hesitate to be as reactionary as the multiplication table. Do not expect to build up the weak by pulling down the strong. Do not hurry to legislate. Give administration a chance to catch up with legislation."

During his years in state and local government, Coolidge reduced the work week, increased workman's compensation, enacted rent control, increased teacher salaries, expanded playgrounds, kept transit fares low, restricted child labor, cared for the mentally ill, and considered whether to seek state-mandated maternity leave. Most of the positions Coolidge took reflected the concerns of his constituents. While a good many of the stands Coolidge took can be attributed to "good politics," in his day, the public was not clamoring for new facilities and programs for the mentally ill and a good many parents, reluctant to forfeit badly needed income, opposed restricting child labor. Coolidge justified his going against or, more appropriately, in advance of public opinion, when he told the Massachusetts State Senate:

"Men do not make laws. They do discover them. Laws must be justified by something more than the will of the majority. They must rest on eternal foundations of righteousness."

Had Coolidge been asked to reconcile his activism as a state official with the more restrained role he as President ascribed to the federal government in redressing social problems, the taciturn Coolidge might have answered with one word, "federalism." Ronald Reagan, who had also been an activist governor, would have heartily agreed. Coolidge, however, sanctioned federal participation in areas in which he had become convinced that states either could or would not discharge what he considered their rightful obligations. For example, Coolidge advocated a federal department of education because he knew that several southern states deprived African-American children access to a decent education on account of their race. In each of his annual messages, Coolidge called upon Congress to exercise its powers of prevention and punishment against the "hideous crime of lynching."

Prior to his Presidency, Coolidge arbitrated settlements in labor disputes often in a fashion favorable to striking workers. Yet he had little tolerance for work stoppages that jeopardized the public. His insistence that "There is no right to strike against the public safety by anybody, anywhere, any time" won him national attention and considerable praise, including from Democratic President Woodrow Wilson. (Many would later draw parallels between Coolidge's action in this instance, and Reagan's firing of the air traffic controllers more than six decades later.)

As he "did the day's work," Coolidge displayed a modesty rarely seen in public figures. Department store magnate Frank Stearns called on State Senator Coolidge for assistance with a sewage disposal bill, but Stearns had been put off by Coolidge's abruptness. "I'm sorry. It's too late," was all Coolidge said. Three years later, however, Coolidge successfully weighed in on the measure without saying a word to the businessman.

Coolidge was at it again, when, as Senate President, he cast the deciding vote against a motion that would have blocked attempts by civil rights leaders to ban the showing of D.W. Griffith's "The Birth of the Nation" in Massachusetts. Riots had broken when the film premiered in Boston. A coalition of nearly

With Mrs. Coolidge hosting a garden party for wounded military veterans at the White House, circa 1924.

Signing appropriations bill for the Veterans Bureau on the White House South Lawn, circa 1924.

two thousand Civil War veterans, clergy and African-Americans marched on the statehouse to protest the film. A bill to set up a three-person censorship board passed the House. When opponents of the measure sought to recommit it, Coolidge broke with his practice of not voting on Senate bills. His "no" vote produced a tie, effectively clearing the path for its passage on the floor. In typical fashion, he said nothing about his action or his reasons for taking it. Nor did he have to. "Coolidge Vote Stops Reconsideration," said one headline. "Opponents of 'Birth of Nation' Win," proclaimed another. Coolidge had done the day's work.

———

The only President born on the Fourth of July, Calvin Coolidge recorded in his autobiography that the United States Constitution, "more than any other document devised by the hand of man" brought so much "progress and happiness to humanity." He saw the system of government the framers established in the Constitution as a consistent and logical embodiment of the universal rights of humanity enshrined in the Declaration of Independence, which preceded the Constitution by 11 years. "Governments do not make ideals," Coolidge said, "but ideals make governments." In an address commemorating the one-hundred fiftieth anniversary of the signing of the Declaration, Coolidge noted that the rights it delineated — liberty, equality and government established by the consent of the governed, all originating from the Creator — were not things that could be touched or seen. That, he believed, is what made them powerful.

As President, Coolidge acted to make those rights more of a reality to all Americans. While Coolidge sometimes fell short, whether through the lack of public support or a want of personal courage, his administration marked a major improvement over those of his predecessors, going as far back to at least Grant. In a "hidden hand" style, anticipatory of the one through which Dwight D. Eisenhower would later operate a half-century later, Coolidge worked behind the scenes to eradicate racial, religious and other injustices brought to his attention. Coolidge, his papers show, acted, primarily through others, to remove vestiges of segregation Wilson had introduced into the federal government. (All would not be gone until Eisenhower's time.) Letters by his two successive chiefs of staff to government officials, informing them that the President wants "this action stopped," "that policy reversed," or "the aforementioned practice terminated," appear in abundance in Coolidge's papers. Most of these interventions stayed out of the newspapers.

For a President known as "Silent Cal," the number of times Coolidge availed himself of the "bully pulpit" of his office to appeal for racial and religious tolerance is noteworthy. When Coolidge was President, the second Ku Klux Klan (owing its founding, in part, to the popularity of "Birth of a Nation") was at its peak and flexing its muscle, boasting a membership of five million. William Henry Lewis, a prominent African-American attorney and an acquaintance of Coolidge from the time both had been undergraduates at Amherst, criticized the President for not denouncing the Klan by name. (Thirty years later, liberals would similarly criticize Eisenhower for not similarly denouncing Senator Joseph R. McCarthy by name all the while the President was resisting McCarthy's tactics and obstructing his investigations.) Taking on such confrontations directly was not Coolidge's way.

As Vice President and as President, Coolidge's practice was to seek out opportunities to show his solidarity with the Klan's intended victims. As Vice President, Coolidge dedicated a hospital for African-American veterans in Tuskegee, Alabama. His closing remarks were, "Those who stir up animosities, those who create any kid of hatred and enmity are not ministering to the public welfare. We have come out of the war with a desire and a determination to live at peace with all the world. Out of a common suffering and a common sacrifice there came a new meaning to our common citizenship. Our greatest need is to live in harmony, in friendship, and in good will, not seeking an advantage over each other but all trying to serve each other."

He hardly intended this as a lesson the hospital's patients needed to learn. After he became president, Coolidge, alerted by the NAACP, William Henry Lewis and others to abuses inflicted on the veterans by a white supremacist staff, directed that an entirely African-American staff replace it. While it would take another world war and the coming to power of another accidental President, Harry Truman, before the armed forces of the United States and its veterans hospitals would be desegregated, Coolidge had been anything but indifferent to the indignities these patients had endured. He had, again, done the day's work.

The year he sought re-election, Coolidge received a letter from a man in New York State protesting the local Republican Party's decision to nominate an African-American man for Congress. "During the war [World War I] five-hundred thousand colored men and boys were called up under the draft, not one of whom sought to evade it," Coolidge wrote back. He went on to inform the writer that the Constitution which he had sworn to uphold "guarantees equal rights to all ... citizens, without discrimination on account of race or color." Coolidge ended his reply with a quotation from a favored predecessor, Theodore Roosevelt: "I cannot consent to take the position that the door of hope — the door of opportunity — is to be shut upon any man, no matter how worthy, purely on the grounds of race or color."

Coolidge, in what had to have been a most unusual move, made this correspondence public, even though he realized that many voters shared the disgruntled citizen's sentiments.

The following summer, in an attempted show of strength, forty-thousand Klansmen and women, marched past the White House en route to a rally on the National Mall. Coolidge was out of town vacationing. The following October he delivered his answer at a gathering in Omaha of the newly formed American Legion. His choice of venue and audience were of significance. Two years earlier, the Klan had wrought considerable chaos upon Omaha, where it had incited racial violence. When a Klan-affiliated majority in the legislature sought to reconvene in a federal building after being barred from the statehouse, Coolidge had denied them access. Before the Legionnaires, Coolidge, the memory of the recent world war much on his mind, called for an immediate "demobilization of racial antagonisms, fears, hatreds and suspicions." Significantly, he titled his address, "Toleration and Liberalism." Coolidge's talk followed others he had delivered before Catholic, Jewish and African-American organizations.

Shortly before President Warren G. Harding's unexpected death, on August 2, 1923, a long-simmering scandal burst out in the open. The "Teapot Dome" affair, which became the most notorious political scandal in American history up to that time, concerned the leasing of government oil reserves at Teapot Dome in Natrona County, Wyoming, and Elk Hill and Buena Vista Hills in Kern County, California, by Harding officials to private interests in the absence of public bidding. While the issuance of such leases was at the time legal, revelations that Interior Secretary Albert Fall had received more than four-hundred thousand dollars (the equivalent of $4 million dollars in 2000), blew the lid off what had to have been the most famous "teapot" in history. While a Senator, Fall had argued vociferously in favor of leasing such reserves to private concerns. Shortly after joining Harding's cabinet, Fall had persuaded the Navy Secretary to transfer jurisdiction of the reserves to the Interior Department, so that he would be able to lease them to oil companies. The unfolding scandal became the first test of Coolidge's leadership.

As he took office, three separate Congressional investigations into what would be known as the "Harding Scandals" were underway. One had as its focus Teapot Dome, another a parallel scandal regarding malfeasance, fraud, featherbedding, kickbacks, and bribery in the Veterans' Bureau, and a third, the lethargy in which Attorney General Harry Daugherty, the unofficial head of Harding's "Ohio gang," had investigated

Sworn in for his second term as Massachusetts Governor, January 8, 1920.

the conduct of his colleagues. Acting on his own accord, Coolidge named two special prosecutors, one a Democrat and the other a Republican, to investigate the corruption within the Executive Branch that he inherited.

Pre-empting Congress from usurping what he regarded as a proper executive function, Coolidge announced on January 28, 1924, that the two counsels would prosecute any wrongdoing within the Executive Branch. "Every law will be enforced," he said, "and every right of the people and the Government will be protected." When Dougherty refused to hand over documents from his files to the Senate Committee investigating Teapot Dome, Coolidge ordered him dismissed. ("The president directs me to notify you that he expects your resignation at once," Coolidge's chief of staff wrote the offending cabinet officer.)

Unlike some of his successors in similar circumstances, Coolidge did not assert "executive privilege," the constitutionally recognized right of one branch of government to prevent another from intruding into its internal operations. (Interestingly, Reagan, following Coolidge's example, waived the same prerogative during the Iran-Contra scandal.) Coolidge replaced the ethically challenged Daugherty with his friend from Amherst days, Harlan Fiske Stone, whom he would later name to the U.S. Supreme Court. (FDR would later elevate Stone to the post of Chief Justice of the United States.)

By May 1924, five months after the full ramifications of what had ensued in the Teapot Dome scandal became public, the scandal was no longer making headlines. Through his decisive action and demonstration of the quality of his character, Coolidge had put the worst of the Harding scandals behind him. His methods closely anticipated those of yet another successor, Gerald Ford, who put an end to an even worse "national nightmare."

A frugal New Englander, Calvin Coolidge was the first President to recognize how excessive taxation can impede economic performance and hamper productivity. Prior to the enactment of the federal income tax in 1913, the entire federal budget had been financed through the collection of excise taxes and tariffs. During the income tax's first years in operation, less than one percent of the population, the wealthiest Americans, paid it. This changed during the First World War, when President Wilson and the war Congress extended its reach considerably. In 1918, individuals earning more than six-thousand dollars (or sixty-thousand dollars in 2000 dollars) paid increasingly higher marginal rates up to a top rate of seventy-seven percent. Along with higher taxes, the federal government borrowed extensively to finance the war. In June 30, 1916, the end of the last fiscal year before the United States entered World War I, the federal debt stood at $1.2 billion (equal to three percent of GDP). After the war, federal debt rose $25.4 billion (equal to nearly thirty-four and nine-tenths percent of GDP) by June 30, 1919.

During a severe post-war recession in 1920, Wilson, in severely poor health and not on the best of terms with a Congress under control of the opposite party, called for tax reductions to stimulate the economy. After campaigning for tax relief in the 1920 election, the Republican Harding appointed Andrew Mellon as Secretary of the Treasury. Mellon pressed the Republican Congress for reductions in marginal individual and corporate income tax rates. Although Congress did not enact all that he and Harding proposed, the Revenue Act of 1921 lowered the top individual income tax from seventy percent to fifty-six percent on income over two-hundred thousand dollars (approximately two million in 2000 dollars), increased personal exemptions, introduced a preferential rate of twelve-and-a-half percent on capital gains, abolished the excess profits tax, but increased the corporate income tax rate to twelve-and-a-half percent.

As the first Vice President to attend cabinet meetings, Coolidge heard Mellon present his case for lower taxes. By the time he became President, he had come to share Mellon's assertion that high tax rates slowed economic growth. Shortly after taking office, Coolidge retained Mellon and directed him to develop plans for additional rate reductions. At Coolidge's request, Congress passed the Revenue Acts of 1924 and 1926. Together, these measures lowered the bottom individual income tax rate from four percent to one and one-tenth percent on income over four-thousand dollars (about thirty-eight thousand nine-hundred fifteen in 2000 dollars), while slashing the top rate to twenty-five percent on income over one-hundred thousand dollars (about nine-hundred seventy-three thousand in 2000 dollars). The 1926 act also abolished the gift tax and slashed the maximum estate tax rate in half to twenty percent. In 1928, the corporate income tax rate was reduced to twelve percent.

Prior to 1921, there had been no such thing as a "federal budget." Each department separately petitioned Congress for its annual appropriations. Harding won Congressional approval to establish a Bureau of the Budget (subsequently renamed during the Nixon administration the Office of Management and Budget). The Bureau reviewed departmental requests and prepared a unified budget for the entire federal government. Coolidge used this process to weed out duplication and waste in federal spending. Armed with this new budgetary tool, Harding and Coolidge together reduced federal debt to $16.9 billion (equal to sixteen and six-tenths percent of GDP) by June 30, 1929.

Through all of these actions, these two presidents ushered in the longest period of prosperity in U.S. history up to their time. (They would be exceeded only by the long expansions of 1960s, 1980s, and 1990s.) As a result of these Mellon-inspired tax cuts, all sectors of the U.S. economy save for agriculture experienced a vigorous recovery throughout the 1920s. Real median income for urban households increased. The number of motor vehicles registered rose from 9.3 million in 1921 to 26.7 million in 1929. High school education became nearly universal. With the enactment of the Harding-Coolidge tax reductions, ninety-eight percent of all Americans paid no income taxes. Perhaps, because of this, the Presidents' critics and political opponents did not deride their tax cuts as "giveaways" to the rich.

On several occasions, Coolidge made clear that he intended these tax cuts not as ends in themselves, but as means to improve the overall quality of life in American society. In 1924, Coolidge told a group of labor leaders that he wanted to tax less so that the people would be able to keep more of their earnings. In his inaugural address of 1925, Coolidge proclaimed taxation in excess of what the government needed to carry out its legitimate purposes "legalized larceny." "The wise and correct course," he said, was for the government to use its taxing powers "not to destroy those who have already acquired success, but to create conditions under which" all would have a "better chance" to be successful.

Repeatedly, he cautioned against the politics of envy. Excessively high tax rates, he argued, produce less revenue, stifle incentive and, inevitably, inflict the greatest harm on those less well off, who reap the burdens of economic slowdowns. In the same speech in which Coolidge, never said, as is still misreported, that the "business of America is business," he set for his vision of what might ensue when the tax code encouraged the accumulation wealth and permitted as much of it to remain in private hands: "Wealth is the product of industry, ambition, character and untiring effort. In all experience, the accumulation of wealth means the multiplication of schools, the increase of knowledge, the dissemination of intelligence, the encouragement of science, the broadening of outlook, the expansion of liberties, the widening of culture … So long as wealth is made the means and not the end, we need not greatly fear it."

While such views came under attack by some of FDR's New Dealers and, later, during the late 1950's when John Kenneth Galbraith, and others, railed against "private affluence and public squalor," they remain the underpinnings of American philanthropy. They also democratized American society by making available and affordable to more people goods and services that had once been among the exclusive preserves of the rich. On the list would be ownership of automobiles, availability of air travel, wider ownership of appliances, mass communication and entertainment, proliferations of museums and scientific laboratories, and access to higher education, to name just a few. This simple Yankee from Plymouth Notch, Vermont had this all figured out — a fact that ranks high among the reasons why he continues to matter.

Alvin S. Felzenberg, Ph.D., is an educator and Presidential scholar. He teaches at the Annenberg School for Communication at the University of Pennsylvania and at the Elliott School of International Affairs at George Washington University. He is the author of *Leaders We Deserved and a Few We Didn't: Rethinking the Presidential Rating Game*.

With Herbert Hoover at the White House during the Hoover inauguration, circa 1929.

HE KNEW WHEN TO SIT IDLE

By John Moser

"For Coolidge, conservatism meant a strict adherence to the Constitution, a tightly limited role for the Executive Branch, and, above all, fiscal discipline."

In his memoirs, Herbert Hoover repeated what he claimed was one of Calvin Coolidge's favorite sayings: "If you see ten troubles coming down the road, you can be sure that nine will run into the ditch before they reach you." Hoover, then Secretary of Commerce, disapproved of this sentiment. The problem, as he saw it, was "that when the tenth trouble reached him he was wholly unprepared and it had by that time acquired such momentum that it spelled disaster."

Hoover was referring to the stock market boom, which, by the start of 1928, had become, in his words, an "orgy of mad speculation." In the past year the amount of money that banks had loaned to brokers for the purpose of making stock purchases had increased by $1 billion. Yet when asked at a press conference whether he thought this amount was excessive, Coolidge responded that there was no reason to believe that the loans were "large enough to cause particularly unfavorable comment."

According to an aide, Hoover was dumbfounded when he learned of Coolidge's statement, although he was a loyal enough Cabinet member to make no public

With Herbert Hoover (undated)

statement to this effect. A little over a year later, after Coolidge had returned to Vermont and Hoover was in the White House, he did exactly what his predecessor had pointedly refused to do — he recommended that the Federal Reserve increase its discount rate, so as to discourage its member banks from putting more money into the hands of stockbrokers.

Was Coolidge less concerned than Hoover about the frenzy of market speculation? The above anecdote would seem to suggest so. But, as historian George Nash has suggested, Coolidge was far less cavalier than he publicly let on. As an individual, he told a family member, he entirely disapproved of what he called "gambling of stocks." Any amount of money that went toward such unproductive purposes was, to his mind, too much. However, he believed that, as President, he lacked the constitutional authority to offer any negative comment. The Federal Reserve, he argued, was a creature of Congress, "entirely independent of the Executive." For him to intervene, even to tender a public opinion on the matter, would be an unwarranted violation of the separation of powers.

This episode offers a perfect illustration of the deep differences in outlook between Calvin Coolidge and his successor in the Oval Office. While both men were lifelong Republicans, their similarities ended there. Hoover was a Stanford-educated cosmopolitan who had spent most of his adult life abroad. By the time Warren Harding tapped him to serve as Secretary of Commerce, he had lived in England, Australia, Burma, China, Bolshevik Russia, and many other locations; he once calculated that he had spent no less than two years of his life at sea. He was also a progressive at heart, supporting the Bull Moose candidacy of Theodore Roosevelt in 1912 and accepting a position in Woodrow Wilson's administration as Food Administrator for post-war Europe. But above all he was an engineer, prone to speaking about efficiency and the need to impose order on a chaotic world. As Secretary of Commerce, he had championed standardization, holding conferences of businessmen in a wide range of industries and getting them to agree on a single size for products from milk bottles to bricks. At a time when most federal agencies were cutting their budgets, Hoover's Commerce Department grew steadily in size. Harding, amazed at his immense energy and his command of statistics, referred to him as "the smartest gink I know." Coolidge, less impressed, simply called him "the wonder boy."

Coolidge had spent his entire career in law and politics, and had only left the country on a single occasion — for his honeymoon, spent in Montreal, Canada. Before becoming President, he had very rarely left his native New England. In sharp contrast to Hoover's constant whirl of activity, Coolidge, who had suffered from a frail constitution since a bout with tuberculosis in his youth, spent up to ten hours a day sleeping. Not only was he a Republican, but a Republican of the type that progressives referred to derisively as "stand-patters"; for example, he had backed William Howard Taft in 1912. Most importantly, he lacked Hoover's urge — likely originating in his background as an engineer — to tinker with the American economy. For Coolidge, as Nash has written, "the purpose of government was not to do good but 'to prevent harm.'"

Coolidge, indeed, was a conservative in the original meaning of the term: a strict adherence to the Constitution, a tightly limited role for the Executive Branch, and, above all, fiscal discipline. Indeed, Hoover remarked that Coolidge was even conservative when it came to fishing; an avid fly fisherman, he was horrified to find that the President insisted on baiting his hooks with worms.

While the relationship between the two men was generally cordial throughout Coolidge's Presidency, the fundamental differences in outlook between them could not help but produce friction from time to

With Herbert Hoover and a delegation from the American Red Cross, circa 1923.

With Mrs. Coolidge, Secretary of Commerce Herbert Hoover and Secretary of State Frank B. Kellogg, Sept. 10, 1925.

time. The President occasionally became annoyed by Hoover's tendency to involve himself in matters that more properly belonged to other cabinet departments; it was not for nothing that some referred to Hoover as "Secretary of Commerce, and under-Secretary of everything else." When asked privately in 1927 what he thought of Hoover, Coolidge allegedly replied, "How can you like a man who's always trying to get your job?" And when the Secretary sponsored a piece of farm legislation that the President opposed, Coolidge angrily barked to his Secretary of Agriculture, "That man has offered me unsolicited advice for six years, all of it bad!"

Nevertheless, after deciding not to seek another term in the White House in 1928, Coolidge made no move to undermine Hoover's quest for the GOP's nomination. The President most likely recognized that there was no other Republican of equal stature, so to oppose his Secretary of Commerce could only help the Democrats. But close observers of politics noted his silence — striking even for "Silent Cal"— during the campaign that year. He refused requests to make speeches on behalf of the campaign, claiming that it was beneath the dignity of his office. Indeed, it was only four days before the general election that he even gave Hoover his formal endorsement, in the form of a telegram to the candidate. It was enough to lead the *New York Times* to ask, "If the President wanted to promote the success of his sometime subordinate, why was he so unconscionably long in bringing himself to do it?"

While the election of 1928 represented another great victory for the Republican Party — one even more decisive than Coolidge's election in 1924 — there would be little continuity between the new President's polices and those of his predecessor. Hoover quickly began pushing for the sort of farm legislation that Coolidge had long opposed, and, while he took no direct actions to check stock market speculation, he repeatedly called on the Federal Reserve Board to increase the discount rate. His activist tendencies became even more pronounced in the wake of the Great Crash of October 1929; he called conferences with business leaders in which the latter promised to cut profits rather than employee wages (a promise that most kept for at least a year), tripled the amount of federal money being spent on public works projects, and organized a massive bailout (in the form of the Reconstruction Finance Corporation) of threatened banks, insurance companies and railroads. Government spending jumped sharply as a result; during the Coolidge years, the federal budget had consistently hovered at just under $3 billion a year, but by 1932, the last year of Hoover's Presidency, it exceeded $4.6 billion. Never in American history had the federal government spent so much during peacetime.

All of this has led historians in recent years to challenge the popular notion of Hoover as a miserly President who callously did nothing while the country was gripped by Depression. More and more they have come to recognize the similarities between Herbert Hoover and his successor in office, Franklin D. Roosevelt. While there were certain lines that Hoover would not cross — for instance, he held out firmly against direct relief payments to the unemployed — many of Roosevelt's initiatives had their origins in policies that Hoover had implemented during his years as Commerce Secretary and President. As prominent Roosevelt advisor Rexford Tugwell put it, "The New Deal owed much to what he had begun."

This recent scholarship suggests that the shift from Coolidge to Hoover was far more profound than the one from Hoover to FDR. But should this not reflect poorly on Coolidge? Was Hoover not correct in suggesting that his predecessor's failure to speak out against speculation on the stock market brought "disaster" to the country in 1929?

Today, of course, most Americans, accustomed to nearly eighty years of activist presidents and a gigantic federal bureaucracy, are inclined to say yes.

But what practical benefit came of Hoover's activism? The Federal Reserve took the new President's advice to raise the discount rate, but this did nothing to stop speculation on the stock market; instead, the resulting contraction in the money supply triggered a recession in mid-1929. While it is impossible to say just what brought about the Wall Street Crash in October, it is hard to imagine that this economic downturn was not a major contributing factor. Moreover, Hoover's subsequent interventions in the economy — government bailouts, attempts to keep wages artificially high in the midst of a shrinking money supply, expansion of public works, a huge tax increase to help balance the budget, and his support for the disastrous Smoot-Hawley Tariff — not only failed to bring recovery, but failed even to check the economy's downward spiral. Many economists claim that these measures made the situation worse than it would have otherwise been.

Coolidge in 1927 reportedly told his Secret Service escort, "They're going to elect that superman Hoover, and he's going to have some trouble. He's going to have to spend money. But he won't spend enough." Eventually, he predicted, "the Democrats will come in and they'll spend money like water. But they don't know anything about money." Sure enough, 1932 saw the election of a new President who was willing to make considerably deeper interventions in the economy than was Hoover. But while Franklin Roosevelt continues to be regarded as one of the greatest Presidents in American history (perhaps deservedly so for his masterful leadership in World War II), there is no getting around the fact that the New Deal did not bring the United States out of the Great Depression. Here again, many economists argue that FDR's activism actually delayed recovery.

Calvin Coolidge did not live to see the New Deal. Ever the party man, he dutifully gave Hoover his public endorsement during the 1932 election campaign. Two months later he was dead. Historians have correctly begun to recognize the continuity between the policies of Hoover and FDR. They have come to see the real break as having come not in 1933, but rather in 1929, when Hoover entered the Oval Office. Perhaps, however, it is time for a serious reassessment of Coolidge's economic policy. Perhaps it was his unwillingness to intervene that deserves our praise, rather than the counterproductive meddling of Hoover and his successors. Now that the historical reputation of the man Coolidge called the "wonder boy" has been at least partially rehabilitated, perhaps it is time to do the same for "Silent Cal."

John Moser, Ph.D., is Associate Professor of History at Ashland University in Ohio. An expert on U.S. Presidents of the early twentieth century, he has written numerous essays and three books on American history: *Presidents from Hoover through Truman, 1925-1953*, *John T. Flynn and the Transformation of American Liberalism* and *Twisting the Lion's Tail: Anglophobia in the United States, 1921-48*. He is currently at work on a book on the history of the 1920s.

Wearing a black armband following the death of President Warren Harding, August 4, 1923.

A QUIET MAN
OF CHARACTER

BY PETER W. SCHRAMM

"Perhaps Coolidge understood that all great truths are simple and they do not very often need a verbose defense."

I met Calvin Coolidge almost forty years ago, while in graduate school. By then I had already been introduced to Lincoln, Jane Austen, Churchill, Shakespeare, and others for whom words mattered, including our Founders. But my prejudice against those with a reputation for being "shy" or "reticent" kept me from introducing myself to Coolidge. It took the efforts of a shy friend, whose own disposition was remarkably similar to that of the former President's, to get me to confront the man and my prejudices. This friend was a student of Coolidge's work and his considered opinion — which I rightly took to be serious — differed from that of the dry-as-dust historian, or the polemicist who pretended to be one. Coolidge, he argued, was deeper than I supposed. There was more to his work — and especially his words — than I imagined.

My friend said many favorable and appealing things about Coolidge — recounting his humble origins, his facility with Latin, his failure at Greek, his lovely and intelligent wife, his attempt to translate Dante on his honeymoon, his dry wit, his ability to debate, his popularity, and his decision not to run for President again

Portrait, May 9, 1924.

— but I only began to pay close attention when my friend repeated Coolidge's words about the Boston police strike: "There is no right to strike against the public safety by anybody, anywhere, anytime." That seemed very clear to me and I was impressed. So I relented to his superior judgment, and I took him up.

So from the beginning, it was Calvin Coolidge's words that grabbed my attention, and his words have continued to hold it ever since. I was less interested in his political actions or the particular decisions made in the various positions he held — including the Presidency — than in the power of his words. The events of a Presidency have as much to do with the measure of any particular President's greatness as do his actions and decisions related to them. And it is fair to say that — when considering the competition — the events of the Coolidge era did not offer much for the staging of greatness. But there is another kind of greatness that can be displayed throughout the ages — no matter what the season or the accidents of fortune. It is greatness of soul. This Coolidge had and this he displayed, most effectively, in his words. Thus it was through reading Coolidge that I came to discover that he was a serious person, an uncommon man.

I also discovered that this shy man was anything but silent. It turned out that he wrote his own speeches, one of the last Presidents to do so. And, although he didn't run for re-election he wrote his own *Autobiography*, something that — up till then — no President since Grant had attempted. His words seemed clean and always clear. Although the prose was spare, it was always straight and true. The simplicity of his expression revealed an honesty and depth — even, perhaps, a manly poetic impulse — that is rare in the political world. Perhaps it is rare everywhere.

I saw his qualities by the time I read less than a dozen pages into his *Autobiography*. Coolidge is remembering a blacksmith his father had hired. He was a "large-framed powerful man with a black beard, said to be sometimes quarrelsome." The boy Coolidge had "seen him unaided throw a refractory horse to the ground when it objected to being shod. But he was always kind to me." Coolidge then explains — do note the cadence and the purity of the sentiment — how the large man would pitch "the hay on the ox cart and I raked after. If I was getting behind he would slow up a little. He was a big-hearted man. I wish I could see that blacksmith again."

This small and particular human picture Coolidge frames with a full heart reveals an honest and straight sentiment that is becoming of a man. When Coolidge penned these words, he was an old man reflecting on a life and a career that spanned several decades and took him to the head of the world's most unique and powerful nation. Yet he recalls this hired man — not just as an equal — but as a man deserving of special recognition on his merits. That man's special kindness toward him was worth remembering because he had learned something important from it. It was worth recounting to others because, in it, there was something for all of us to learn about ourselves and about our character as a people.

What stands out most remarkably in Coolidge's writing is his democratic sentiment; his democratic soul, if you will. What I mean by that is his marked devotion — in principle, in words and, above all, in action — to the idea that we are all equal before God. Coolidge is not to be praised for his lack of snobbery with the blacksmith. The absence of snobbery is to be expected. The mere concession of talking to and cheerfully working alongside a hired man (or even the giving up of one's seat on a wagon to a hired girl) does not make a man a great democrat. What made Coolidge a great democrat and a great man was his willingness to recognize the merit in such people. His ability to look beyond what good manners required and to confront the man as a man — to see his graces, to recognize his charity, and to take the lesson in as readily as he might have done were it offered by a schoolmaster rather than a blacksmith — this distinguishes Coolidge's democratic sentiment from a more aristocratic, duty-bound sense of equality. Coolidge did not do this man a favor in recognizing him; indeed, he recognized that it was he — Coolidge — who had received the favor.

Coolidge later came to understand — perhaps he always sensed it — that this true democratic sentiment (as opposed to a faux democratic sentiment that amounts to nothing more than benign aristocracy masquerading as concern for the masses) is the thing that made America great. On the occasion of the one-hundred fiftieth anniversary of the Declaration of Independence, he put it this way: "We live in an age of science and of abounding accumulation of material things. These did not create our Declaration. Our Declaration created them." In other words, our greatness as a people came from our devotion to true democratic sentiment — a sentiment that paved the way for every man to rise to his level best and put no artificial impediments on anyone.

Throughout the *Autobiography* there is also a notable silence regarding what many may regard as Coolidge's highest achievement as President: the great prosperity the country enjoyed during his Presidency. But as with so many of Coolidge's silences, there is a deeper meaning and an attachment to democratic sentiment that explains it. Coolidge did not understand himself to be responsible for that prosperity in the direct sense. The industry of the people and their collective devotion to the principles enshrined in their Declaration had made it possible. "Our Declaration created them," he insisted.

People tend to confuse charity with democratic sentiment. This is a mistake. Charity is a sentiment born of our inequalities, not our equality — it is the sentiment felt by the strong for the weak. Charity is, nevertheless, a quality that all good men — no less democratic men — should foster. After all, it was charity that led the blacksmith Coolidge described to "slow up a little" when young Calvin got behind. Coolidge recognized that this man's charity ennobled him — even as it reminded Calvin of his own inferiority. Coolidge honored the blacksmith's charity with gratitude and respect. It placed the man somewhat higher in Calvin's estimation than he was in the common opinion of other citizens. In saying that he wished he could see that man again — as he was an older and accomplished man — he was recognizing a meritorious kind of equality between them. This man's equality with Coolidge before God and under the law meant — not only that the blacksmith was owed the ordinary courtesies of citizenship — but also that this blacksmith was a potential friend. The blacksmith's virtue had proven it.

Yet Coolidge has this reputation for silence and — as with most prejudices — it must have its roots in some kernel of truth, even if that truth is wildly misunderstood. There are places in the *Autobiography* where Coolidge's silences are striking — especially to a modern ear. But they are too striking not to be deliberate and, if deliberate, they must be meaningful. Though democratic sentiment is certainly part of what is at work in Coolidge's meaningful silences, there is also humility and cheerful resignation. Humility, in turn, is certainly related to democratic sentiment — as is a cheerful focus on the good. Consider his admission that he cannot describe his own mother; and even his assertion that no man is really equal to the task of describing his mother. Although she lived, more or less, as an invalid for much of her life, Coolidge does not fail to see the essential nobility that bubbled under the surface: "There was a touch of mysticism and poetry in her nature," and, "Whatever was grand and beautiful in form and color attracted her." He may not have been up to the task of giving her a full description, but his focus was — nevertheless — on something good and high in her nature. He did not dwell in the low or the negative or the sad. She died at age thirty-nine and, about that, Coolidge simply writes: "The greatest grief that can come to a boy came to me. Life was never to seem the same again." He might have indulged in, and the reader would have forgiven him, much more raw emotion on this life-altering and soul-wrenching event. A modern reader might wish to read more evidence of brooding — for such readers mistake brooding for depth. But, really, what more could be said to make his statement more powerful or to make it convey a better sense of the tragic?

Coolidge makes note of his education in the law — which came from a kind of apprenticeship at a firm rather than in a law school. He admits his partiality to that method, but does not fail to give reasons to support his prejudice. In the tutelage of that firm and through his own study of summary student law books (rather than the

College-era portrait taken while he was a student at Amherst College, undated.

With Presidential Secretary Edward T. Clark, circa 1923.

too comprehensive law books used in the office), he prepared his mind for the real practice of law. This combination of practical wisdom and summary study gave him a broader view and a power to grasp the essential in situations. It helped him to avoid diversion into tangential points or unnecessary, though interesting, anecdotes. He makes the reader smile as he states an opinion that lawyers just as often fail to give an adequate accounting of the facts as they fail to give an adequate accounting of the law. That is because, we assume, they have not adequately honed their powers of perceiving the essential. Perhaps it is this skill that is most wonderfully reflected in his beautiful economy with words.

Yet another example of Coolidge's mastery of the language (and of his composure) is given in his statement about the devastating loss of his sixteen-year-old son Calvin, from blood poisoning due to stubbing his toe while playing tennis on the lawn. Coolidge wrote: "In his suffering he was asking me to make him well. I could not. When he went the power and the glory of the presidency went with him." And here his democratic soul is (yet again) re-awakened; this time in its impotence. There are few things that make one feel his limitations more keenly than an inability to help one's own child. In these moments we must recognize — no matter what heights we have scaled — that there are things that are equally beyond our control as they are beyond the control of the lowest among us. No matter how great he was, this proved that he was still just a man.

About a third of the way into the *Autobiography*, we meet Coolidge as a student at Amherst. By his account, his first two years were not especially interesting and he even considered leaving if he did not find a way to distinguish himself and, thereby, justify his father's expense. But then things began to click. At last he began both to enjoy and to profit from his labors. The turning point seems to have come when he met the man who taught the course that, it seemed to him, "all our other studies were in the nature of a preparation for." This man was Charles E. Garman and the course was philosophy.

In the next few pages Coolidge attempts to give the reader a good and a clear accounting of what Garman taught, how he brought the students together in intellectual fellowship, and what a deep effect this man had on all his students. Garman's Socratic method seemed to etch the eternal things on the hearts and minds of his students. Coolidge had him for four terms.

Garman was not a scholar. He published nothing. But he was an inspiring teacher, in the oldest and best sense of the term. He was entirely devoted to the subject at hand and to the students who attempted to understand it, and was "one of the most remarkable men with whom I ever came in contact." He wrote and printed pamphlets — just for his students — which "he pledged us to show to no one outside the class, because, being fragmentary, and disclosing but one line of argument which might be entirely demolished in succeeding lessons, they might involve him in some needless controversy. It is difficult to imagine his superior as an educator." And then the former President gives his teacher the final honor: "Truly he drew men out."

This is yet another powerful Coolidge-ism. "Truly he drew men out." If one reflects on it, one sees that it says much more than it seems to say. Garman drew "men" out. He drew them out of their shell. He made them "men." He "drew" them out. That is, he coaxed something out of them that was, really, already there. He did not "draw" them in the sense of creating or impressing his will upon them. He tested their mettle and saw what kind of men they were. He gave them assignments that encouraged them to think independently and together. And, in this summary of Garman from Coolidge, we get the sense that Coolidge believes this was the essential and wonderful thing about his teacher. Garman was, in a sense, Coolidge's beau ideal of a democratic statesman: a teacher, a mentor and a friend.

Garman taught classes in psychology, philosophy and ethics. He was both a man of character and a follower of the truth. It seems important for Coolidge to note that Garman taught him about "the nature of habits and the great advantage of making them our allies instead of our enemies." He showed the students that "man is endowed with reason, that the human mind has the power to weigh evidence, to distinguish between right and wrong and to know the truth." Coolidge then writes, "While the quantity of the truth we know may be small it is the quality that is important. If we really know one truth the quality of our knowledge could not be surpassed by the Infinite."

Coolidge explains that Professor Garman stressed learning "thorough mastery and careful analysis" of all the arguments on any subject under consideration. Coolidge writes, "We were not only learning about the human mind but learning how to use it, learning how to think. A problem would often be stated and the class left to attempt to find the solution unaided by the teacher. Above all we were taught to follow the truth whithersoever it might lead. We were warned that this would oftentimes be very difficult and result in much opposition, for there would be many who were not going that way, but if we pressed on steadfastly it was sure to yield the peaceable fruits of the mind. It does."

Coolidge writes, "We looked upon Garman as a man who walked with God." Furthermore, his course was a demonstration of "the existence of a personal God, of our power to know Him." It is important for Coolidge to know that "every reaction in the universe is a manifestation of His presence," and the conclusions that follow therefrom: "It sets man off in a separate kingdom from all other creatures in the universe, and makes him a true son of God and a partaker of the Divine nature." And this has special political and moral significance for Coolidge because, "This is the warrant for his freedom and the demonstration of his equality. It does not assume all are equal in degree but all are equal in kind. On that precept rests a foundation for democracy that cannot be shaken. It justifies faith in the people."

True democratic sentiment — that is, the seeing of potential friends in all comers unless and until proven otherwise — comes from the recognition of that big, but simple truth. It comes from the cheerful recognition that we're all in the same boat, so to speak. We are all better than dogs and, yet, still much less impressive than God. And the possession of that knowledge brings with it a kind of quiet dignity. Coolidge evinces this most clearly when he summarizes his view of the teachings he absorbed with Garman's assistance. He gives a clear, even vivid accounting of them, but it is matter-of-fact. He is not naïve about the reception this description is likely to get in some quarters and he notes that many will see it and think it simplistic. He has no use for this criticism. "With them," he says, "I have no argument. I know that in experience it has worked. In time of crisis my belief that people can know the truth, that when it is presented to them they must accept it, has saved me from many of the counsels of expediency. The spiritual nature of men has a power of its own that is manifest in every great emergency from Runnymede to Marston Moor, from the Declaration of Independence to the abolition of slavery." Perhaps Coolidge understood that all the great truths are simple and they do not very often need a verbose defense. Coolidge's words were sparing because the truth doesn't need ornamentation. Like the Declaration itself and like Lincoln's best defense of it — the Gettysburg Address — Coolidge's writing reflected the simple grandeur of American independence and its commitment to a liberty born of equality.

This clear account of the basis of popular government is expanded upon in his "Speech on the Occasion of the One Hundred and Fiftieth Anniversary of the Declaration of Independence." In this remarkable speech he is able to connect both the theological and philosophical modes of thinking regarding equality and the "great mystery of how to live." He is persuasive as he lays out the meaning of the political axiom of "the doctrine of equality" and why the liberation of America also meant the ennobling of humanity. Coolidge wants us to remember our country's birthday because we should set aside a time to "think the thoughts that" the Founders thought. We are tempted to think in terms of "results and effects," but he thinks, "It is to the cause that we must ascribe our results." We cannot neglect and abandon the

With his family dog, circa 1927.

cause and continue to enjoy the result. Our character as a nation depends on this understanding and our actions resulting.

July 4, 1776 is regarded "as one of the greatest days in history" because for the first time a nation was established on new principles. Thus it is the case that the Declaration of Independence becomes "the most important civil document in the world." It asserts and understands something critical about the nature of mankind "and therefore of government." All men are created equal and are endowed with certain inalienable rights "and that therefore the source of the just powers of government must be derived from the consent of the governed."

And for Coolidge this massive fact is in line with the "laws of human nature," as well as the "religious convictions" of Americans. The preachers of the day could preach equality and support popular government because "they believed in the fatherhood of God and the brotherhood of man." The Declaration is both profoundly American as well as a great spiritual document. It is the product of both their political thought and religious life. Coolidge reminds us that we live "in an age of science and of abounding accumulation of material things. These did not create our Declaration. Our Declaration created them. The things of the spirit come first."

And he reminds us to connect the individual rights of the Declaration with consent and that this theory plays itself out in the Constitution, which "guarantees our liberty" by separating powers and balancing the interests of the three branches of the government, "with checks against each other in order that neither one might encroach upon the other." The Constitution tries to assure that government by consent does not "degenerate into the unrestrained authority of a mere majority or the unbridled weight of a mere influential few."

There is one paragraph worth quoting from the speech in full because it reveals more perfectly Calvin Coolidge's turn of mind and how he is able to reveal it to his fellows. The reader will note not only the Anglo-Saxon cadence in the paragraph, but also how it does something to the reader — how it brings his whole soul into activity, thus proving that the so-called "silent" Cal knew something deep about both the language and the character of his people:

"About the Declaration there is a finality that is exceedingly restful. It is often asserted that the world has made a great deal of progress since 1776, that we have had new thoughts and new experiences which have given us a great advance over the people of that day, and that we may therefore very well discard their conclusions for something more modern. But that reasoning can not be applied to this great charter. If all men are created equal, that is final. If they are endowed with inalienable rights, that is final. If governments derive their just powers from the consent of the governed, that is final. No advance, no progress can be made beyond these propositions. If anyone wishes to deny their truth or their soundness, the only direction in which he can proceed historically is not forward, but backward toward the time when there was no equality, no rights of the individual, no rule of the people. Those who wish to proceed in that direction can not lay claim to progress. They are reactionary. Their ideas are not more modern, but more ancient, than those of the Revolutionary fathers."

Peter W. Schramm, Ph.D., is Executive Director of the John M. Ashbrook Center for Public Affairs and Professor of Political Science at Ohio's Ashland University, where he is also Chairman of the Master's Program in American History and Government. He has written on Calvin Coolidge, Abraham Lincoln and Booker T. Washington. Formerly, he was President of the Claremont Institute for the Study of Statesmanship and Political Philosophy.

Seated in the Oval Office, August 15, 1923.

HE EXEMPLIFIED COMMON SENSE

By David M. Shribman

"In a period when the entire country was making a great, reckless wager in hopes of a great fortune, Coolidge personified thrift and prudence."

So has there ever been a President so well understood and yet so misunderstood, so easy to categorize and yet so difficult to pigeonhole, so quotable and yet so often described as taciturn, so identified with one state and yet propelled to national office from another, so much a caricature of one century's values and so adaptable to another century, so much an exemplar of rural America and yet so dependent for his national reputation upon an episode in urban America?

We can only be speaking of Calvin Coolidge, the son of Vermont who ascended to the Presidency from Massachusetts, the man who piled up firewood in his farmhouse and who piled up accolades for his posture in the Boston police strike, the man who never said much of anything but who is remembered, often incorrectly, for some of the signature American remarks about business, conservatism and the reluctance to run for office.

Calvin Coolidge is like the seersucker suit, never in style but never quite out of style either. In his White House years, he did not exactly match the go-go optimism of

On the farm at Plymouth Notch with sons, John and Calvin, and his father, John, undated.

the roaring stock market, nor the new post-war self-confidence of America, nor the prevailing zeitgeist of personal and financial risk. In a period when the entire country was making a great, reckless wager in hopes of a great fortune, Coolidge personified thrift and prudence. At a time when the country was full of boosters and boasters, Coolidge defined humility. At a time when the very notion of fashion was in fashion, Coolidge was unfashionably unfashionable.

But now, more than three-quarters of a century after his Presidency, there are a few hints that Mr. Coolidge of Plymouth Notch, Vermont, might be inching back into fashion, and not because, perhaps alone with Bill Clinton, we know something about his underwear (CC's was baggy). Today, we like a man who speaks his mind. Today, we like a man who is silent when silence is called for. Today, we like a man who stands up. Today, we like a man who knows when to be seated. Today, we like a man who tells it straight, without artifice, without flowery excess. Today, we like a story like the one about how, at 2:47 on a dark August morning, he was sworn into the office of the Presidency by the light of a kerosene lamp and by his father, who was of course a Notary Public, and proud of it. This is still an American story, perhaps the greatest American story, and surely the greatest American story ever to feature a Notary Public.

I admit to being a late convert to the Coolidge cult, though I also admit to having the zeal of the convert. I grew up in his adopted state — more than that, I grew up in the very beach town where he *summered*, a decidedly un-Coolidge verb — but I ingested the usual stereotype, that Coolidge was a rusticated simpleton of few words and no good ideas or virtues. Like much of what I thought when I was young, I was wrong. In maturity I discovered that Coolidge was quite a different character than the one I imagine; indeed that Coolidge was, above all, all about character. And that, far from being a simpleton, he was the symbol of simple truths. Big difference there.

Coolidge was smart, articulate, brave. He was the personification of the rectitude of the county clerk: exact, deliberate, fair, accurate in all respects. He was a family man, and in truth suffered dearly the loss of his son, and none of us can doubt Coolidge when he said of the death of Calvin Coolidge, Jr., in 1924, that at that moment "the power and the glory of the Presidency went with him." I keep on my desk, for no particular reason but as a reminder of the poignancy and poetry of Coolidge, a copy of the President's hand-written inscription in Coolidge's volume *Have Faith in Massachusetts* that resides in the library of Dick's House at Dartmouth College, the infirmary named for another young man who died too young: "To Edward K. Hall, In recollection of his son and my son who have the privilege by the grace of God to be boys through all eternity."

No man without a soul could have written those lines, nor the other Coolidge remark that I have loved since my days in college, his tribute to Vermont as the state he loved. If you think of Coolidge as the ultimate man of prose, consider what he said in 1928 of the great Vermont flood, remarks that probably were spontaneous, as the true poetry of his heart: "Vermont is a state I love. I could not look upon the peaks of Ascutney, Killington, Mansfield and Equinox without being moved in a way that no other scene could move me. It was here that I first saw the light of day; here I received my bride; here my dead lie, pillowed on the loving breast of our everlasting hills." No wonder that for generations Vermont third graders have been asked to memorize this little speech, a kind of Gettysburg Address of the north.

Claude M. Fuess, an Amherst historian, wrote perhaps the best biography of Coolidge, and he was right when he concluded, "Among Calvin Coolidge's fine qualities, two stand out above all others — common sense and sound character." These are not common virtues, and yet they are what we seek, every four years, when we set out to choose a President.

Accepting his Presidential nomination, circa 1924.

Abraham Lincoln and Calvin Coolidge are seldom represented in the same sentence, but I think it is incontrovertible that Coolidge and Lincoln are our best exemplars of those two qualities of common sense and sound character. Throw in the bedrock sense of integrity that both men possessed and you have kind of a White House trifecta.

Read Coolidge's speeches and you will find that he did not mean what the folklore says he meant when he remarked that the business of America was business (he went on to say, and no one quotes this part: "Of course the accumulation of wealth cannot be justified as the chief end of existence"). Nor did he mean what the public thinks he meant when he urged listeners to be as reactionary as the multiplication table (the sentence that preceded that remark: "Don't hesitate to be called as revolutionary as science").

He did mean this one, however, taken from the same 1914 speech as the remark about the multiplication table: "Do the day's work." In the end, President Coolidge is the President who bid America to do the day's work. There was nothing of the theory of the leisure class to Calvin Coolidge. He did the day's work.

David M. Shribman is the Executive Editor of the *Pittsburgh Post-Gazette*. Formerly he was Washington bureau chief of *The Boston Globe*, national political correspondent for *The Wall Street Journal*, and a political and Congressional reporter for *The New York Times*. Shribman was awarded the Pulitzer Prize in 1995 for his coverage of Washington and the American political scene. He is an emeritus member of the Board of Trustees of Dartmouth College and of the Board of Visitors of the Nelson A. Rockefeller Center for the Social Sciences at Dartmouth.

Receiving an original parchment of President Abraham Lincoln's Gettysburg Address, presented by The Italian Republican League of New York February 12, 1927.

HISTORICAL FACTS

Vital Statistics:

Ancestry: English, some Indian blood

Religion: Joined Congregational Church in 1923

Height: 5'10"

Weight: 169 pounds

Hair: Red

Presidential salary: $75,000

Professional History:

Read the law in the firm of John C. Hammond and Henry P. Field in Northampton, Massachusetts from 1895 to 1898.

Admitted to the Massachusetts Bar in July 1897.

Opened own law office in Northampton, Massachusetts in February 1898.

Political career began as Northampton City Councilman in 1898.

Served as Northampton City Solicitor, City Republican Chairman and Clerk of the Courts, Hampshire County.

Elected to Massachusetts General Assembly 1906, re-elected 1907.

Elected Mayor of Northampton 1909, re-elected 1910.

Elected to State Senate, 1911, 1912, 1913, and 1914; served as Senate President last two terms.

Elected Lieutenant Governor of Massachusetts in 1915, 1916, and 1917.

Elected Governor of Massachusetts in 1918 and 1919; consolidated 118 different state departments into 18.

Ended the Boston Police Strike of September 1919 with the firing of 1,100 striking officers, and restored public safety by hiring approximately 1,500 replacement officers from a pool of unemployed World War I veterans.

Nominated in June of 1920 for Vice President of the United States on the Warren G. Harding ticket.

Succeeded to the Presidency on August 3, 1923, after Harding died in San Francisco.

Elected to the Presidency in 1924; Charles G. Dawes his Vice President.

Inaugural Address first to be broadcast on radio.

Announced, "I do not choose to run for president in 1928," in August 1927 and left the Presidency in March 1929.

In retirement wrote his autobiography, magazine articles and a syndicated newspaper column.

Served as President of the American Antiquarian Society from 1929 to 1933.

Served as a director of the New York Life Insurance Company.

MEMBERS OF THE COOLIDGE CABINET:

Secretary of State - Charles Evans Hughes (1923-25); Frank B. Kellogg (1925-29)

Secretary of the Treasury - Andrew W. Mellon (1923-29)

Secretary of War - John W. Weeks (1923-25); Dwight F. Davis (1925-29)

Attorney General - Harry M. Daugherty (1923-24); Harlan F. Stone (1924-25); John G. Sargent (1925-29)

Postmaster General - Harry S. New (1923-29)

Secretary of the Navy - Edwin Denby (1923-24); Curtis D. Wilbur (1924-29)

Secretary of the Interior - Hubert Work (1923-28); Roy O. West (1929)

Secretary of Agriculture - Henry C. Wallace (1923-24); Howard M. Gore (1924-25); William M. Jardine (1925-29)

Secretary of Commerce - Herbert C. Hoover (1923-28); William F. Whiting (1928-29)

Secretary of Labor - James J. Davis (1923-29)

TAX AND DEBT REDUCTION ACCOMPLISHMENTS:

National debt of $22.3 billion in 1923 lowered to $16.9 billion by 1929.

Federal expenditures of $5.1 billion in 1921 were reduced to $3.3 billion in 1929.

Cut taxes four out of his six years as president.

Cut effective tax rate on the wealthy from 50 percent (1922) to 20 percent. Revenue from that tax bracket then rose from $77 million to $230 million.

By 1927, 98 percent of the population paid no income taxes.

Tax burden on those making under $10,000 fell from $130 million in 1923 to under $20 million in 1929.

INDUSTRY ACCOMPLISHMENTS:

Unemployment averaged 3.3 percent from 1922 to 1929.

Gross National Product increased annually by 7 percent from 1924 to 1929.

Per capita income grew 30 percent from 1922 to 1928.

Real earnings for employed wage earners increased 22 percent from 1922 to 1928.

Industrial Production increased 70 percent from 1922 to 1928.

The average workweek decreased 4 percent from 1922 to 1928.

Automobile production grew threefold.

FOREIGN POLICY ACCOMPLISHMENTS:

Favored U.S. participation in the World Court.

Opposed U.S. participation in the League of Nations.

Avoided war with Mexico and restored diplomatic relations.

Withdrew U.S. troops from Nicaragua.

Non-recognition of the Soviet Union.

Attended the International Conference of American States in Havana.

PEACE PACTS AND TREATIES:

Dawes Plan for Reparations (1924)

Kellogg-Briand Pact (1928)

OTHER PRESIDENTIAL HIGHLIGHTS:

Vetoed the Bonus Bill for Veterans.

Presided over prosecution of Harding Era scandals; restored trust in Presidency.

Signed the Immigration Act of 1924.

Signed legislation making Indians U.S. citizens.

Proposed increased funding for aviation.

Proposed construction of the St. Lawrence Seaway.

Appointed Harlan Fisk Stone to the Supreme Court in 1925.

Signed the Jones-White Act of 1928 for construction of merchant ships.

Signed the Federal Radio Act, creating Federal Radio Commission.

Proposed an anti-lynching law and a federal Department of Education and Relief.

Released the remaining Sedition Act violators convicted during the Wilson administration.

Designated $250 million to construct public buildings resulting in Washington D.C.'s Federal Triangle.

Dedicated Mount Rushmore.

Authorized construction of Hoover Dam.

Twice vetoed the McNary-Haugen Farm Bill.

NOTABLE NATIONAL EVENTS DURING PRESIDENCY:

Charles Lindbergh flies solo across the Atlantic.

National Prohibition — rise of Al Capone.

Scopes Evolution Trial.

Leopold & Loeb Murder Case.

First radio network (NBC) forms.

"The Jazz Singer" debuts — talkies replace silent films.

Notable in Music: George Gershwin, Louis Armstrong, Paul Whiteman, Guy Lombardo, Al Jolson.

Notable in Business: Henry Ford, Walter Chrysler, Harvey Firestone, Samuel Insull.

Notable in Journalism: H. L. Mencken, George Jean Nathan, Harold Ross, Henry Luce.

Notable in Sports: Babe Ruth, Red Grange, Jack Dempsey, Gene Tunney, Helen Wills, Bill Tilden.

Notable on Film: Charlie Chaplin, Rudolf Valentino, Clara Bow, Lon Chaney, Douglas Fairbanks.

Notable on Broadway: Eugene O'Neill, Flo Ziegfeld, Fannie Brice, Will Rogers, the Marx Brothers.

CHRONOLOGY

1872

July 4 - John Calvin Coolidge is born in Plymouth Notch, Vermont.

1885

March 14 - Victoria Josephine Moor Coolidge, Calvin's mother, dies at age 39.

1890

March 6 - Abigail G. Coolidge, Calvin's sister, dies at age 14.

May 23 - Graduates from Black River Academy, Ludlow, Vermont. Secretary of Class. Gives speech entitled "Oratory in History."

1891

September 17 - Begins studies at Amherst College, Amherst, Massachusetts.

1895

June 26 - Graduates magna cum laude from Amherst College. Classmates vote for Calvin to give the "Grove Oration," a humorous address. Calvin Coolidge drops 'John' from his name (although he continues to sign letters to his father 'J. Calvin Coolidge). Begins law studies in Northampton, Massachusetts.

December 13 - Wins gold medal from Sons of the American Revolution in a National Essay Competition for "The Principles Fought For in the American Revolution."

1897

July 2 - Gains entrance to the bar in Northampton, and later is appointed to the Republican City Committee from Ward 2.

1898

Opens his law office.

December 6 - Appointed Northampton City Councilman from Ward 2.

1900

January 18 - Elected Northampton City Solicitor.

1902

January 16 - Defeated for Northampton City Solicitor by Theobald M. Connor.

1903

June 4 - Appointed Clerk of Courts of Hampshire County, Massachusetts.

1904

Meets Grace Anna Goodhue.

1905

October 4 - Marries Grace Anna Goodhue at Burlington, Vermont.

December 5 - Defeated for Northampton School Committeeman by John J. Kennedy.

1906

September 7 - Birth of John Coolidge, first child.

November 6 - Elected Representative to the Massachusetts General Court.

1908

April 13 - Birth of Calvin Coolidge, Jr., second child.

1909

December 7 - Elected mayor of Northampton, beginning a continuous course of public service to March 4, 1929.

1911

November 7 - Elected Massachusetts State Senator.

1913

November 4 - Reelected Massachusetts State Senator and subsequently elected President of the Senate.

1914

January 7 - Delivers "Have Faith in Massachusetts" address to the Massachusetts Senate.

November 3 - Reelected State Senator and President of the Senate.

1915

May 12 - Sixty-five Amherst alumni meet at the Algonquin Club in Boston to honor Senator Coolidge as a fellow alumnus.

November 2 - Elected Lieutenant Governor of Massachusetts.

1918

November 5 - Elected Governor of Massachusetts at the age of 47.

1919

January 2 - First Inaugural Speech as Governor of Massachusetts: "Reflections on WWI."

September 9-11 - Comes to national attention because of his stand for law and order during the Boston Police Strike.

November 4 - Reelected as Governor of Massachusetts.

1920

June 12 - Nominated for Vice President of the United States by the Republican National Convention as Warren G. Harding's running mate.

November 2 - Elected Vice President of the United States.

1921

March 4 - Warren G. Harding inaugurated as President, Calvin Coolidge as Vice President, of the United States.

1923

August 3 - Upon news of President Harding's death in San Francisco, Coolidge is sworn in as President by his father, a Notary Public, in the homestead at Plymouth, Vermont.

1924

> Coolidge appoints special legal council to investigate scandals such as the "Teapot Dome."

> June 2 - Coolidge signs bill making Indians citizens of the United States.

> June 12 - Nominated for President of the United States at the Republican National Convention in Cleveland.

> July 7 - Calvin Coolidge, Jr., second son, dies at Walter Reed Hospital from blood poisoning.

> November 4 - Elected President of the United States.

1926

> March 18 - Colonel John Coolidge, father, dies.

1927

> June 11 - Meets with Lindbergh and awards Distinguished Flying Cross.

> August 2 - From summer White House at Rapid City, South Dakota, issues statement, "I do not choose to run for President in 1928."

> August 10 - Dedicates work on Mt. Rushmore.

1928

> January 16 - Gives address at Sixth Annual International Conference of American States in Havana, Cuba.

> August 27 - Signs the "Pact of Paris," also known as the Kellogg-Briand Pact, considered at the time a significant forward step in international relations. The pact is ratified by the U.S. Senate and signed by President Coolidge on January 17, 1929.

1929

> March 4 - After attending the Inauguration of President Herbert Hoover, Mr. and Mrs. Coolidge return to Northampton, Massachusetts to live.

> May - *The Autobiography of Calvin Coolidge* is published.

1933

> January 5 - Calvin Coolidge dies at age 60 in his Northampton home from a coronary thrombosis.

ABOUT THE NATIONAL NOTARY ASSOCIATION

The National Notary Association, founded in 1957, is the leading authority on the American Notary office and is recognized nationally and internationally for its work regarding notarial customs, laws, practices and ethics.

As the largest organization serving the nation's 4.8 million Notaries, the nonprofit professional Association supports a membership that represents every U.S. state and jurisdiction — and in many other countries — by promoting best practices that bolster consumer protection, and by inspiring Notaries to uphold their important role as deterrents to fraud.

Working to preserve the national public trust, the NNA also promotes understanding about the Notary's important role and duties in society. It has drafted and published the *Model Notary Act* to help lawmakers introduce effective legislation, and established *The Notary Public Code of Professional Responsibility* — a comprehensive standard for ethics, best practices and professional conduct.

Through its nationally accredited educational programs and member benefits, the NNA provides the guidance Notaries need to comply with state laws, rules and requirements; to safeguard themselves and their employers from liability; to manage risk to prevent fraud and identity crimes; to perform professionally at the highest ethical standards; and to take advantage of opportunities that arise out of elevated levels of training and qualification.

Inspired by the thirtieth President of the United States, who set an example of unimpeachable personal integrity and character, the NNA honors government officials who heighten the professionalism and effectiveness of the American Notary Public office through its prestigious Calvin Coolidge Notary Award.

ABOUT THE NATIONAL NOTARY FOUNDATION

Established in 1997, the National Notary Foundation is the independent philanthropic arm of the National Notary Association and provides support to a variety of educational, charitable and humanitarian programs on behalf of the nation's 4.8 million Notaries. By backing the academic and personal achievement of young people, along with donating critical assistance to those in need across the country, the Foundation promotes the values and ideals of the NNA and Notaries, which includes dedication to public service and helping the less fortunate.

Notaries know firsthand about worthwhile causes and public service, and, through the humanitarian and philanthropic work of the Foundation, Notaries inspire others to follow a charitable course.

The Foundation endows scholarships and grants at colleges and universities throughout the country and continues to seek out opportunities to benefit education in the name of NNA members. In so doing, the Foundation is a beacon of education, scholarship and self-improvement, and a prominent symbol of the Notary Public's essential role of service to the community.

Additionally, NNF donations have benefitted medical research and victims of natural and other disasters both domestic and abroad.

The National Notary Foundation is a nonprofit corporation established exclusively for charitable and educational purposes under Internal Revenue Service Code 501(c)(3).

ABOUT THE CALVIN COOLIDGE MEMORIAL FOUNDATION

The Calvin Coolidge Memorial Foundation, Inc. was established in 1960 as a nonprofit educational organization to preserve the legacy of America's thirtieth President, Calvin Coolidge, and to redress the fact that there is no Presidential library for him. The Foundation is the only membership organization devoted to President Coolidge, and its mission is to inspire the public to appreciate and study his legacy — his personal life, values, and ideals, and his public career — in order to understand our nation's history and to forge a stronger democratic society for the future.

The Foundation develops and publishes materials and programs about Coolidge and provides primary and interpretive information by request to the media, students, scholars, genealogists and the general public. The Foundation owns and maintains its offices in Plymouth Notch, Vermont, and holds memberships in the Association of State and Local Historical Societies, the New England Museum Association and the Vermont Museum and Gallery Alliance.

The Calvin Coolidge Memorial Foundation, Inc., is an educational nonprofit 501(c)(3) organization.